CALUMET CITY PUBLIC LIBRARY

3 1613 00515 5067

W9-BVM-247

Mexico

J
972
SON

Mexico

BY LIZ SONNEBORN

Enchantment of the World™
Second Series

CALUMET CITY
PUBLIC LIBRARY

CHILDREN'S PRESS®

An Imprint of Scholastic Inc.

Frontispiece: **San Ildefonso Cathedral, Mérida**

Consultant: Luis Urrieta Jr., Associate Professor, Curriculum & Instruction, Mexican American Studies, University of Texas at Austin
Please note: All statistics are as up-to-date as possible at the time of publication.

Book production by The Design Lab

Library of Congress Cataloging-in-Publication Data
Names: Sonneborn, Liz, author.
Title: Mexico / by Liz Sonneborn.
Description: New York : Children's Press, an imprint of Scholastic Inc.,
   [2018] | Series: Enchantment of the world | Includes bibliographical
   references and index.
Identifiers: LCCN 2016054005 | ISBN 9780531235706 (library binding)
Subjects: LCSH: Mexico—Juvenile literature.
Classification: LCC F1208.5 .S637 2016 | DDC 972—dc23
LC record available at https://lccn.loc.gov/2016054005

No part of this publication may be reproduced in whole or in part, or stored in a retrieval system, or transmitted in any form or by any means, electronic, mechanical, photocopying, recording, or otherwise, without written permission of the publisher. For information regarding permission, write to Scholastic Inc., 557 Broadway, New York, NY 10012.

© 2018 by Scholastic Inc.
All rights reserved. Published in 2018 by Children's Press, an imprint of Scholastic Inc.
Printed in the United States of America 113
SCHOLASTIC, CHILDREN'S PRESS, and associated logos are trademarks and/or registered trademarks of Scholastic Inc., 557 Broadway, New York, NY 10012.

1 2 3 4 5 6 7 8 9 10 R 27 26 25 24 23 22 21 20 19 18

Cowboy in Guadalajara

Contents

Left to right:
**Popocatépetl,
Parachicos dancers,
Guadalajara
Cathedral, fishers,
Mayan girl**

CHAPTER 1

The Day of the Dead

EVERY YEAR, AT THE BEGINNING OF NOVEMBER, many people in Mexico celebrate Día de los Muertos, or the Day of the Dead. Some dress up in costume, decorate their homes with images of skulls and skeletons, and tell stories about the spirits of those who have died. On the surface, the holiday seems to have much in common with Halloween as celebrated by people in the United States, the country directly to the north of Mexico. But in fact, the two holidays are very different in tone and meaning.

Even with its scary tales and spooky decorations, Halloween is a lighthearted holiday, focusing mostly on costumes, candy, and trick-or-treating. The Day of the Dead, though festive, is much more serious. During the multiday celebration, many Mexicans interrupt their daily routine to remember beloved relatives and friends they have lost.

Opposite: **Brightly painted skulls are common decorations during the Day of the Dead.**

MARIA SALUD
GUILLEN E
22-NOV-12
20-ABR-05

JESUS PEÑA
1904-11-DIC. 1999

Marigolds are the most common flower used to decorate graves for the Day of the Dead. It is said that their bright orange color and strong scent help lead the spirits back home.

Bringing the Dead Home

The Day of the Dead is said to be the one time of the year when the spirits of the dead can come back to earth and visit the living. But according to the tradition, the spirits will only return if their relatives pay proper tribute to them. Some Mexican families construct altars to guide their dead loved ones home. These altars are decorated with flowers, candles, and photographs of the deceased. They also often feature *papel picado*, pieces of colorful tissue paper with designs of human skulls cut out of them.

Families also set out food and drink because the spirits are likely to be hungry and thirsty after their long journey home. There might be clay bowls of tamales or enchiladas and glasses of water or mugs of hot chocolate, all depending on what the dead liked most when they were alive. Often special treats are placed at the altars. For example, a child's altar might include a candy bar or a bag of potato chips.

Two treats frequently displayed are sugar skulls and *pan de muerto*. Sugar skulls are small decorated candies in the shape of a skull. Pan de muerto, meaning "bread of the dead," is a sweet bread with sugar sprinkled on top. Sometimes the bread is molded into the shape of a laid-out corpse with its hands crossed over its chest.

Many families work hard to create an altar that will please the dead. They worry that if they do not properly fulfill their responsibilities to the dead, they may become ill or suffer a spate of bad luck. They also want to impress their neighbors with their dedication to their loved ones.

At the Gravesite

For many Mexicans, the celebration of the Day of the Dead also includes a trip to a cemetery. Carrying brooms, flowers, and food, families arrive at the gravesites of relatives. After cleaning the area and the tombstones, they adorn the graves with flowers, usually bright yellow marigolds.

People then feast while praying or swapping stories about the deceased. One person might recite a *calaverita*, a poem to honor the dead. A family member might wave over one of the mariachi bands wandering through the cemetery. In exchange for a small tip, these traditional bands will play a favorite song.

Sometimes, groups of relatives spend the entire night at the cemetery. Sharing this time together, with the smell of flowers and the sound of music swirling around, they can once again feel the presence of the loved ones who are no longer with them.

A Public Event

Traditionally, celebrating the Day of the Dead was a family and community affair. But increasingly, it is becoming a more public event. The Zócalo, a large square in the historic part

On the Day of the Dead, families sit at the graves of their deceased relatives, sometimes all night long.

of Mexico City, is adorned with great arches of marigolds to welcome the dead. Local governments also sponsor altars constructed in public spaces. Banks, supermarkets, and other shops set up their own altars as holiday decorations.

Day of the Dead processions and street festivals are also becoming more popular. Many people who attend these festivals wear costumes. In particular, women dress up as La Calavera Catrina, or the Elegant Skull, a character taken from the art of José Guadalupe Posada. To depict La Catrina, women put on white face paint and sketch a black skeletal grin around their mouth.

Not everyone in Mexico likes how the Day of the Dead has changed. Some people are annoyed that Mexican children have embraced certain Halloween traditions. They might

Mexican painter Diego Rivera's mural *Dream of a Sunday Afternoon in the Alameda Park* depicts much of Mexican history. This detail shows, from left to right, a self-portrait of Rivera; the artist Frida Kahlo, who was Rivera's wife; La Calavera Catrina; and José Guadalupe Posada, the artist who created the character of La Catrina.

dress up in playful costumes and carry orange plastic pumpkins, asking passersby to toss coins inside. But even with the adoption of some American customs, the Day of the Dead remains a uniquely Mexican celebration. It combines elements of Mexico's history with attitudes toward death that arise from the country's often complex and difficult past.

Creating the Holiday

The Day of the Dead had its origins in the Aztec Empire. The Aztecs were one of several indigenous, or native, peoples who lived long ago in what is now Mexico. They were a powerful people, who took control over neighboring groups by force. In the Aztec world, many religious rituals focused on death and dying. The Aztecs made offerings of food and flowers to the dead. They also performed overnight ceremonies at gravesites and decorated the skulls of enemies killed in war.

In the early sixteenth century, the Aztecs' lands were invaded by Europeans. Spanish soldiers took over the Aztec Empire and stole the Aztecs' wealth. They created a new society where the Spanish were on top and the Aztecs were on the bottom.

The Spanish were Roman Catholics, and the priests wanted the Aztecs to convert to their religion. To maintain elements of their religions, the surviving Aztecs incorporated traditional death rituals into the celebration of two Catholic holidays—All Saints' Day (November 1) and All Souls' Day (November 2). The result was the Day of the Dead. Since life under Spanish rule was hard for the indigenous people, the

yearly celebration of the dead helped them deal with their mistreatment and sorrow and envision an afterlife.

The tradition of La Calavera Catrina also grew out of the Mexican people's struggles. By the early twentieth century, most Mexicans were poor. A small group of rich people held tight control over society and politics. Posada's images of the finely dressed Catrina made fun of the rich. It reminded people that the rich were just like the poor in one important way—death would one day take them all.

Young couples dress as La Calavera Catrina for a Day of the Dead parade in Morelia, a city to the northwest of Mexico City.

The inevitability of death has been a theme running through much of Mexican history. Mexicans won their independence from Spain, but only after a long, violent war during which many people died. And establishing Mexico as a nation pitted various groups against each other, causing even more deaths. Mexico has largely been at peace for many decades. But the violent upheavals of the past remain deeply embedded in the hearts and minds of its people.

A Uniquely Mexican Holiday

The Day of the Dead reflects Mexico's history. During the festivities, Mexicans refuse to see death as scary or sad. Like their difficult past, death is something they look at not with horror, but with clear-eyed honesty and humor.

The great Mexican writer Octavio Paz maintained that his people were unique in their matter-of-fact acceptance of death. He wrote, "The Mexican . . . frequents it, mocks it, caresses it, sleeps with it, entertains it, it is one of his favorite playthings and his most enduring love."

Paz's words could also apply to how many Mexicans feel about their native land. There are painful memories of Mexico's past that still hurt them. There are problems with their country today that still frustrate them. But, despite it all, Mexico remains their most enduring love.

Young people walk through the historic streets of Guanajuato, a city in central Mexico. Many Mexicans are excited about the ways the country is changing, while still being proud of its past.

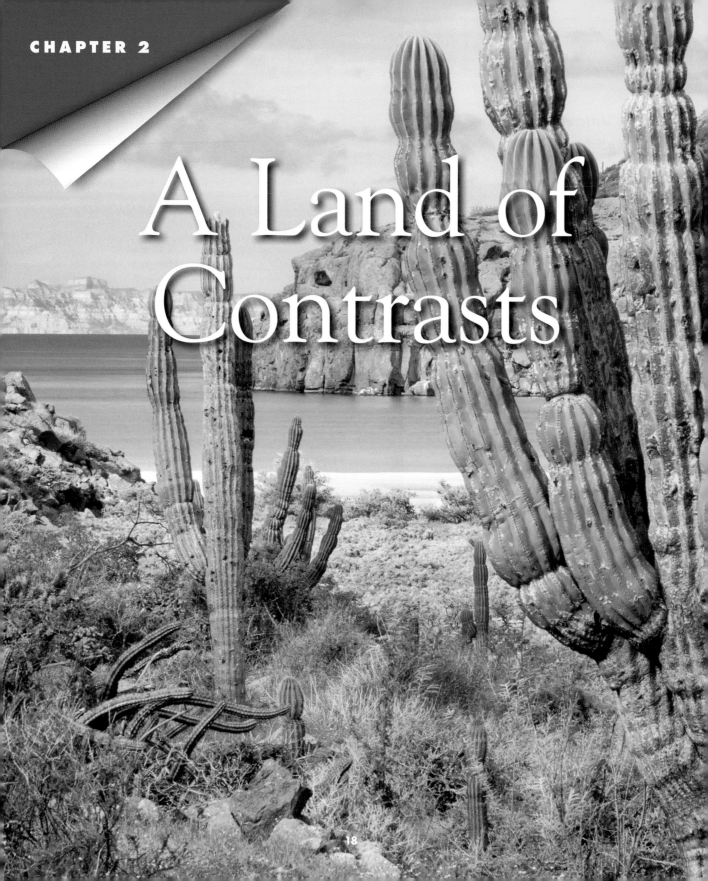

CHAPTER 2

A Land of Contrasts

M

EXICO IS A NATION OF MANY LANDSCAPES. It has high plateaus and low coastal plains. It has wet rain forests, dry deserts, and snowcapped mountains. People in different regions of the country are likely to be surrounded by environments that might seem worlds apart, even though they are in the same country.

Opposite: **The desert meets the sea in Baja California, in northwestern Mexico.**

Mexico's Neighbors

Mexico is part of the continent of North America. Its neighbor to the north is the United States. Mexico lies just to the south of the U.S. states of California, Arizona, New Mexico, and Texas. To the south, Mexico shares borders with the countries

Mexico's Geographic Features

Area: 758,449 square miles (1,964,375 sq km)

Highest Elevation: Pico de Orizaba, 18,619 feet (5,675 m) above sea level

Lowest Elevation: Laguna Salada, 33 feet (10 m) below sea level

Largest Island: Tiburón Island, 464 square miles (1,202 sq km)

Largest Lake: Lake Chapala, 417 square miles (1,080 sq km)

Longest River: Rio Grande (Río Bravo del Norte in Mexico), 1,896 miles (3,051 km)

Longest Border: With the United States, 1,960 miles (3,155 km)

Average High Temperature: In Mexico City, 81°F (27°C) in May; 72°F (22°C) in December

Average Low Temperature: In Mexico City, 54°F (12°C) in May; 43°F (6°C) in December

Average Annual Precipitation: 28 inches (71 cm) in Mexico City

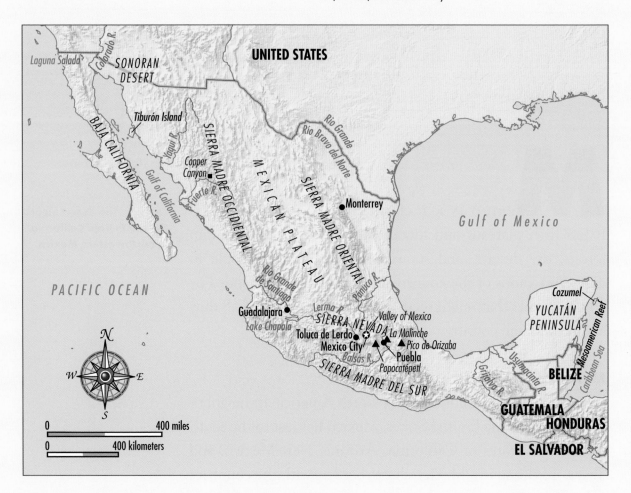

The Rio Grande serves as the boundary line for roughly a third of the border between Mexico and the United States.

of Guatemala and Belize. To the east and to the west, Mexico butts up against bodies of water. Its eastern coast borders the Gulf of Mexico and the Caribbean Sea, parts of the Atlantic Ocean. Its western coast lies along the Pacific Ocean.

Mexico is a fairly big country. It covers an area of 758,449 square miles (1,964,375 square kilometers), making it the fourteenth-largest nation in the world.

Rivers and Lakes

A river defines much of the country's northern border. The river is called Río Bravo del Norte in Mexico. In the United States, it is known as the Rio Grande.

About 150 other rivers also flow through Mexico. Most empty into the Pacific Ocean. About one in three of them

People who live in villages near Lake Chapala have long fished in the lake. The water has become polluted, however, and the number of fish in the lake has dropped dramatically.

flows into the Caribbean Sea or the Gulf of Mexico. Major rivers in Mexico include the Grijalva, Usumacinta, Pánuco, and Balsas.

Mexico is also the site of a large number of lakes. The country's largest lake is Lake Chapala. In recent years, many American and Canadian retirees have moved to communities around the lake.

The Mexican Plateau

Running north to south in the middle of Mexico is a great plateau. A plateau is an area of flat land at a high elevation. The Mexican Plateau ranges from about 3,000 feet (900 meters) to 8,000 feet (2,400 m) above sea level. The elevation is lowest in the north and gradually rises moving south.

Life in Mexican Cities

With one-sixth of the Mexican population, Mexico City is by far the country's most important urban center. But Mexico also has other large vibrant cities with exciting attractions of their own.

Guadalajara (below), with a population of 4,843,000, is Mexico's second-largest city. Located close to the center of the country, it is a significant industrial hub. Goods made there include building materials, soft drinks, and handicrafts. One of its most distinctive buildings is the Degollado Theater, where audiences can enjoy plays, operas, and dance performances. Some of the best-known features of traditional Mexican culture, including mariachi music and sombreros, originated in Guadalajara.

Monterrey in the northeastern part of the country is home to about 4,513,000 people. Settled by the Spanish in 1579, it is Mexico's most important busi-

ness center today. Many Mexican and international corporations have headquarters there. One of its most famous landmarks is the Lighthouse of Commerce. At night, this 230-foot-tall (70 m) red monument beams a green spotlight across the city sky.

Lying at the foot of Popocatépetl, a great snow-capped volcano, is Puebla (above). Home to 2,984,000 people, it is located southeast of Mexico City. During the French occupation of Mexico, a small group of soldiers defended the city against French forces on May 5, 1862. Their victory is now celebrated on the holiday Cinco de Mayo. Long known for its pottery, the city is also famed for its Talavera ceramic tiles, which decorate many of its buildings. Other products manufactured in Puebla include glass and textiles.

Cable cars carry visitors over the spectacular Copper Canyon in the northern Mexican Plateau. Copper Canyon gets its name from the color of its walls.

The northern portion of the Mexican Plateau is largely hot and dry. Most of the people there live near irrigated farms. In more barren areas, ranchers raise cattle and other animals.

The southern portion of the Mexican Plateau is far more hospitable. Since ancient times, it has been the center of Mexican life. The majority of the Mexican population lives there. The Central Plateau is also home to many of Mexico's largest cities, including its capital of Mexico City. Much of Mexico's agricultural, industrial, and mining wealth is made in this important region.

The Mountains of Mexico

The Mexican Plateau is flanked by two mountain ranges that run much of the length of the country. To the west is the Sierra Madre Occidental. To the east is the Sierra Madre Oriental, an extension of the Rocky Mountains that run through the western United States.

The two ranges come together south of Mexico City to form a belt of mountains running east to west across the middle of the country. This is known as the Trans-Mexican

Volcanic Belt or the Sierra Nevada. These mountains include Pico de Orizaba, Mexico's tallest peak and the third-highest mountain in North America.

Like many other nearby mountains, Pico de Orizaba is a volcano. But it has not erupted for more than 150 years. A much greater threat is the active volcano Popocatépetl, whose name means "smoking mountain." Popocatépetl frequently spews ash, and a major eruption could put the lives and property of some thirty million people at risk.

Farther south, the Sierra Madre del Sur runs along the Pacific Ocean. These mountains reach elevations of about 7,000 to 8,000 feet (2,100 to 2,400 m).

The Coastal Plains

Low-lying plains line both coasts of Mexico. In the west, the lowlands include the coast of Baja California. This long, narrow strip of land is one of the longest peninsulas in the

La Malinche

High above the city of Puebla rises La Malinche. This majestic volcano is named after one of the most controversial people in Mexican history.

In 1519, Spanish soldiers led by Hernán Cortés arrived in what is now Mexico. After the Spaniards won a battle with a group of Mayas, they took twenty young women captive. One of them was Malinalli (or Malintzin), later known as La Malinche. She was particularly valuable to the Spaniards because she knew Nahuatl, the language of the Aztec people who then ruled central Mexico. She was forced to act as a translator for Cortés in his campaign to conquer the Aztec Empire for Spain. La Malinche also had a son by Cortés.

For a time, La Malinche was celebrated as a founding mother of Mexico, but later Mexicans came to see her as a traitor to her people. Today, *malinchista* is an insult hurled at Mexicans who reject their own culture and embrace the ways of foreigners. But recently, many Mexican and Mexican American women have come to appreciate La Malinche for her resilience and survival.

Ash billows from
Popocatépetl. On clear
days, the volcano can be
seen from Mexico City.

world. It is separated from the rest of Mexico by the Gulf of California. Along the northern coast of this gulf, the land is part of the Sonoran Desert, which stretches into Southern California and Arizona.

The lowlands of eastern Mexico lie on the coast of the Gulf of Mexico and the Caribbean Sea. The oil-rich port of Veracruz is located there. The coast and nearby islands also feature many of the country's most beautiful beaches. Tourists flock to resorts in the city of Cancún and on the island of Cozumel.

The Yucatán Peninsula juts into the Gulf of Mexico in the southeastern part of the country. The northern side of the Yucatán Peninsula is a dry, flat plain, while the southern portion is hot and rainy. This area is covered with tropical rain forests. Coral reefs are found along its marshy coast.

Temperature and Rainfall

Given the size and terrain of Mexico, it is not surprising that the climate varies from place to place. The northern desert registers the highest temperatures. But the Yucatán and the coastal plains are also hot much of the year. The northern part of the Mexican Plateau, where its elevation is the lowest, is hotter than the southern reaches of the plateau, where the elevation is higher.

Mexico City is usually comfortable, no matter the season. April is the hottest month, with the temperature rising to an average of 80°F (26.5°C). The average high temperature in January, the coldest month, is not much lower at 70°F (21°C).

Rainfall also varies across Mexico. Much of the country is fairly dry. The northern and central parts of the Mexican Plateau are semiarid. They only receive about 12 inches (30 centimeters) of rain a year. The southern plateau, where Mexico City lies, is wetter. It receives more than twice the annual rainfall that the

More than thirty million foreign tourists visit Mexico every year. Many come to relax on the nation's beautiful, warm beaches.

Southern Mexico is the wettest part of the nation. In towns such as San Cristóbal de las Casas, rain is common, especially in the summer months.

northern plateau receives. The coastal plains receive a fair amount of rain, especially the northern Gulf Coast. It usually gets between 10 and 24 inches (25 and 61 cm) of precipitation each year.

Mexico is vulnerable to hurricanes. These violent storms are more common on the Gulf and Caribbean coasts than they are on the Pacific coast. Hurricanes come with strong winds and often high seas and heavy rain that produce severe flooding and other damage. In 2005, Hurricane Wilma struck the Yucatán Peninsula, causing billions of dollars in damage.

Environmental Concerns

The Mexican government is also concerned about damage to the environment caused by humans. One problem is deforestation. Some forests have been cut down to clear land for farming and ranching.

Other major sources of concern are water and air pollution. In urban areas, sewage often contaminates the water supply and car exhaust poisons the air. Air pollution is particularly a problem in Mexico City. The nearby mountains prevent the dirty air from blowing away and mixing with cleaner air from other places. Many people in the capital have trouble breathing because of the polluted air.

The Mexican government recognizes pollution as an important problem. Nevertheless, it often fails to approve the funding needed to protect both people and wildlife from this continuing threat.

Xochimilco

On Sunday afternoons, thousands of locals and tourists flock to Xochimilco, just outside of Mexico City. There, they while away hours, meandering through a network of canals in brightly colored boats called *trajineras*. During their boat rides, visitors admire the beautiful flowers and plants growing on the islands they pass by.

But Xochimilco is not just a weekend destination. It is also one of the only remnants of the system of canals and islands built by the ancient Aztecs. The Aztec capital of Tenochtitlán was located on top of several interlocking lakes. The Aztec people created islands there called *chinampas*. They placed a frame made of cane in the water and covered it with rich mud from a lake bottom. In the mud, they farmed crops. In time, roots grew down to the lake floor, locking the chinampas in place.

The Spanish drained most of the lakes of Tenochtitlán. Xochimilco is one of the only places where chinampas remain intact. But even these are now threatened. Polluted water is damaging the area's ecosystem. Many Mexicans fear that unless the government steps in to save Xochimilco, its beautiful islands and canals will soon be destroyed.

CHAPTER 3

Into the Wild

MEXICO'S WILDLIFE IS JUST AS VARIED AS ITS terrain. It is one of the most biologically diverse countries in the world. Within Mexico's borders, there are an astounding twenty-six thousand species of plants. Its animal population includes some five hundred species of mammals, one thousand species of birds, and 1,200 species of reptiles and amphibians.

Opposite: **The jaguar is the largest predator in Mexico. Jaguars can adapt to a wide variety of habitats, from rain forest to desert.**

Plant Life

The deserts of northern Mexico are too dry for many types of vegetation, but some grasses and shrubs thrive there. Because they can survive with little water, hundreds of types of cacti also grow in these desert lands.

One unique plant in Mexico is the boojum tree. It is found only in the desert of Baja California and the Mexican state of

A towering boojum tree in Baja California

Sonora. The boojum can grow as high as 60 feet (18 m). Its trunk tapers toward the top, making it look something like a giant carrot planted in the dirt. From base to tip, the trunk is covered with little spiky branches that sprout small green leaves and, in the summer, tiny cream white flowers. The boojum grows very slowly and can live for hundreds of years.

Forests once covered much of the Central Plateau and the Sierra Madre Occidental. But many of these trees have been cut down. However, pine forests still cover the higher elevations of the Sierra Madre Occidental range, while some oak forests are found at lower areas.

Mexican's lushest vegetation grows in its tropical rain forests. In this hot, moist region, mahogany trees, ferns, and palms are plentiful. Many types of orchids, which have colorful and fragrant flowers, also grow wild.

The Dahlia

In 1963, Mexico named the dahlia as its national flower. Dahlia plants produce showy, brightly colored flowers with many petals. Dahlias had long flourished on the country's high plateaus. Dahlia plants probably grew in the royal gardens of Aztec emperor Montezuma II.

The dahlia was little known outside of Mexico until the late 1700s. At that time, an expedition of Spanish scientists was collecting specimens of Mexican plants. The scientists sent dahlia seeds to the Royal Botanical Garden in Madrid, Spain. Botanists throughout Europe began cultivating this spectacular flower and creating new varieties. There are now about thirty species of dahlia plants. Sprouting beautiful blooms of white, yellow, red, and purple, they are popular with gardeners the world over.

The swampy Pacific coast of the southern state of Chiapas features many mangrove trees. The mangroves protect inland areas from the winds and rains of hurricanes. Many fruit trees grow in southeastern Mexico. These trees produce mangoes, papayas, guavas, and pomegranates. Another product from this region is chicle. This ingredient in chewing gum comes from the chicozapote tree.

Mammals

Northern Mexico once teemed with wild animals, large and small. Many small animals such as rabbits, armadillos, skunks, and snakes still live in the rugged land. But as Mexicans transformed the natural habitat into ranches and farms,

The northern tamandua is a type of anteater that lives in Mexico. It spends most of its time in trees, where it uses its long tongue to lick up ants and termites.

larger animals were pushed out. Ranchers brought in cattle to replace them. Rural Mexicans also kept burros, small donkeys used to carry goods.

Wild deer, coyotes, foxes, and bears found a new home in more mountainous areas not suited to ranching. They share their lands with the peccary, a stout, piglike animal. Mountain lions live there as well.

Other types of wild cats inhabit Mexico's rain forests. They include the jaguar, puma, and ocelot. The agile margay is especially suited to living in trees. Its wide paws allow it to run up tree trunks and even hang upside down from strong branches.

The rain forests are also full of spider and howler monkeys. The howler monkey gets its name from its loud cry, which can travel as far as 2 miles (3 km). Other rain forest dwellers include tapirs and anteaters.

With 5,795 miles (9,330 km) of coastline, Mexico is also home to many marine mammals. Gray whales swim in the waters off Baja California, while sea lions and seals live along both coasts. The rare vaquita is found only in the Gulf of California. With a population of just over fifty, this small porpoise is now in danger of extinction.

Mexico's National Animals

Mexico does not have just a single national animal. Instead, the country bestows this honor on six different creatures.

National mammal: The jaguar, the largest cat in North America, is known for its fierceness. The animal was featured in the myths of the ancient Aztecs, Mayas, and other indigenous peoples of what is now Mexico.

National marine mammal: The vaquita is a species of porpoise that lives only in the Gulf of California. Its name is Spanish for "little cow."

National bird: The golden eagle has a wingspan of 7 feet (2 m). An image of this great bird appears on the Mexican flag.

National dog: The xoloitzcuintli, or xolo (top left), is also called the Mexican hairless. One of the breed's two varieties has no fur; the other has a very short coat.

National reptile: The green turtle (bottom left) nests on beaches along Mexico's coast. Once considered endangered, the turtle's population has grown in recent years because of conservation efforts.

National insect: The grasshopper is known by the Nahuatl word *chapolin* in Mexico. Toasted grasshoppers, flavored with garlic or chilies, are a favorite snack among some Mexicans.

Collared lizards grow to about 14 inches (36 cm) long. They get their name from the two black stripes around their neck.

Sea Life, Reptiles, and Birds

The warm water of the Gulf of Mexico is ideal for coral reefs. Found off the coast of the Yucatán Peninsula, the Mesoamerican Reef is the second-largest coral reef in the world. The reef provides a home for hundreds of types of sea life, including fish, turtles, and sharks. The reef is a favorite destination for divers and snorkelers.

Both the east and west coasts of Mexico are nesting grounds for sea turtles. Of the seven species of sea turtles, six are found along Mexico's shores. They include the leatherback sea turtle, one of the biggest reptiles in the world.

The Morelet's crocodile is another large reptile found in Mexico. It dwells in the swamps of the Yucatán. The Morelet grows to about 9 feet (3 m) long and can live to be eighty years old.

In northern Mexico, lizards are a common sight. They range in size from the mighty iguana, which grows as long as humans are tall, to the tiny gecko, which can fit in the palm of a person's hand. The Mexican collared lizard is one of the country's most unusual reptiles. Using its tail for balance, this lizard can run upright on its back legs.

Many types of snakes slither through Mexico. Some rattlers, vipers, and constrictors are dangerous to humans as well as their animal prey. Much less menacing is the Mexican vine snake. It can grow more than 6 feet (2 m) long but is as skinny as a pencil. The vine snake lives in forests. Colored brown

The Bat Man of Mexico

Rodrigo Medellín, a professor at the National Autonomous University of Mexico, has spent decades trying to save Mexico's endangered species. His most recent cause is the lesser long-nosed bat. His work has earned him the nickname the Bat Man of Mexico.

Mexican farmers have long relied on the lesser long-nosed bat to pollinate blue agave plants. The blue agave is used to make tequila, a popular alcoholic drink that is an important Mexican export product. In recent years, some agave growers have been cutting off the plants' flowers to increase its sugar content. This eliminated a source of the bat's food, putting its survival in danger.

To save the bat, Medellín persuaded agave farmers to let some of their plants grow the natural way. Not only is this traditional farming method better for the bats, but it also protects the agave crop. The bats eat insects that might otherwise destroy the plants.

Male quetzals are notable for their long tail streamers. These brilliant green feathers extend more than twice as long as the rest of the bird.

and green, it can easily hide from predators. Wrapped around a tree trunk, it looks like a branch.

Birds live throughout Mexico. Common types of birds include hawks, eagles, buzzards, and hummingbirds. Bright pink flamingos inhabit the swamplands of the Yucatán. Many other brilliantly colored birds, such as the macaw, the toucan, and the quetzal, live in the rain forests. The quetzal was sacred to both the ancient Mayas and Aztecs. The male sports a bright red breast and long green feathers on top of its tail.

The Gulf Coast is also the winter home of many migratory birds. More than three million ducks and geese arrive there from the north when the weather turns cold.

Saving Wildlife

Mexico has a variety of habitats where plant and animal life can thrive. But many people are concerned that some habitats are being damaged or destroyed. The rapid growth of cities endangers wilderness areas. Deforestation and pollution are also great threats to animals and plants in the wild.

Trees Full of Butterflies

Every fall, the trees in the Mexican state of Michoacán turn orange. It is not because their leaves change colors. The trees are instead completely covered with twitching orange-and-black monarch butterflies.

Monarchs live in the United States east of the Rocky Mountains. But when the weather turns cold, they take a 2,500-mile (4,000 km) journey to central Mexico. To stay warm, they cluster together on pine and oak trees.

In 1980, Mexico created the Monarch Butterfly Biosphere Reserve in Michoacán. The forests of this area are preserved so the migrating monarchs will always have a place to spend the winter.

The Mexican government is trying to preserve some natural habitats. About 13 percent of the country is protected as parks and nature reserves. These protected areas include a wide range of landscapes and habitats. Montes Azules Biosphere Reserve in southern Mexico is a vast area of tropical forest where more than five hundred species of trees grow. Desert meets sea at El Vizcaíno Biosphere Reserve in Baja California. The reserve protects the coastal dunes, mangrove swamps, nearby waters, and the wildlife that lives there.

Despite government efforts, many conservationists are still concerned about the future of Mexico's wildlife. A large number of Mexican animal species are endangered. If more is not done, animals such as the quetzal, jaguar, and spider monkey may one day become extinct.

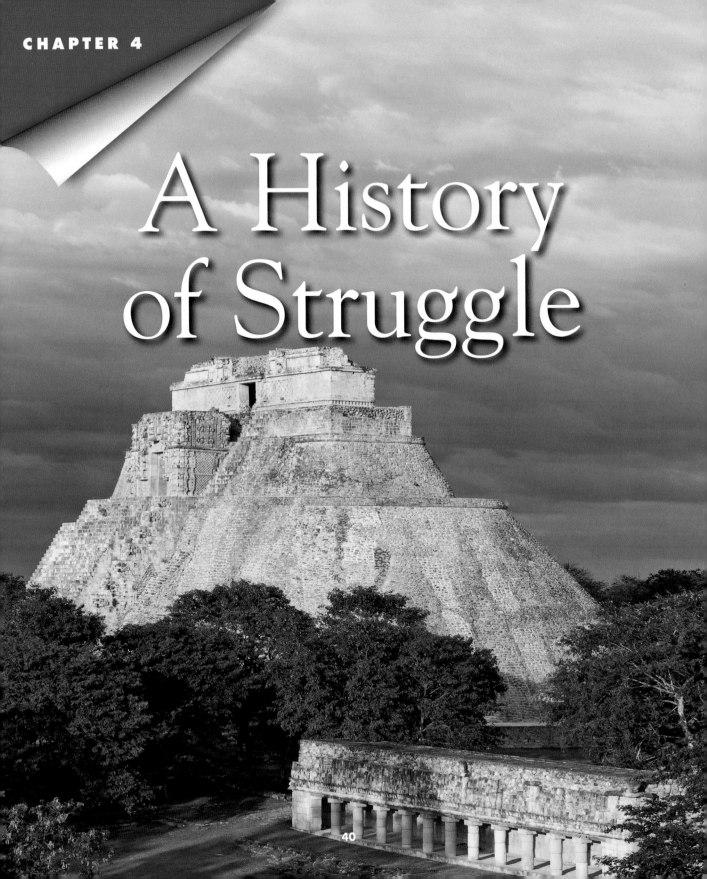

CHAPTER 4

A History of Struggle

EVERYWHERE IN MEXICO, THE PAST IS IN PLAIN sight. There are pyramids and temples left behind by ancient civilizations. There are churches and buildings constructed during the country's three centuries under Spanish rule. There are murals, painted by some of Mexico's greatest artists, depicting its people, both the powerful and the powerless, building their shared nation through time.

The history of Mexico is a story full of conflict and despair. But it is also a story of defiance and triumph that fills Mexicans with pride and binds them together as a people.

Mexico's First Peoples

Human beings were living in what is now Mexico by 15,000 BCE, and possibly earlier. These first peoples survived by hunting large animals. Because of changes in the climate, later

Opposite: **The Mayas built massive pyramids that towered above the thick forests. Construction began on the Pyramid of the Magician, at Uxmal on the Yucatán Peninsula, in the sixth century CE.**

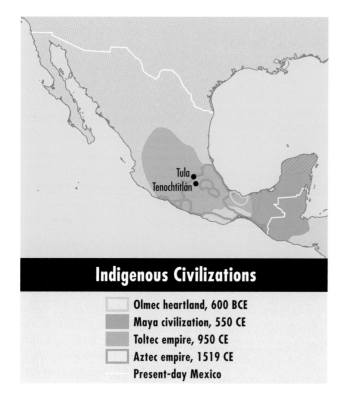

Indigenous Civilizations

Olmec heartland, 600 BCE
Maya civilization, 550 CE
Toltec empire, 950 CE
Aztec empire, 1519 CE
Present-day Mexico

inhabitants relied on hunting small game and gathering wild plants.

By about 9000 BCE, early peoples began to farm. They grew corn, beans, squash, peppers, and other food crops. Needing to live near their fields, they began to build settlements. Small farming villages grew into urban centers with large populations.

A series of advanced civilizations emerged in what is now Mexico. The Olmecs along the Gulf Coast established a large trade network and crafted enormous sculptures. The Mayas of the Yucatán Peninsula built great stone pyramids and developed a sophisticated writing system. The Toltecs in the Valley of Mexico established the large capital city of Tula and created a mythology centered on the feathered serpent god Quetzalcoatl.

Olmec Heads

The best-known artifacts of the Olmec culture are the colossal sculptured heads found at several archaeological sites. These large heads measure as high as 11 feet (3 m) and weigh as much as 30 tons (27 metric tons). The sculptures were likely portraits of the faces of Olmec rulers. Olmec sculptors did not have metal tools. They instead used stones to carve their artworks from massive slabs of dark gray basalt.

The Rise of the Aztecs

The last great civilization of early Mexico was that of the Aztecs, sometimes called the Mexicas. In 1325, the Aztecs founded their capital of Tenochtitlán in what is now Mexico City. By conquering other peoples, they established a vast empire. Tenochtitlán eventually grew to have a population of between two and three hundred thousand. Tenochtitlán was one of the largest cities in the world at that time.

The Aztecs also developed a complex culture. Their society included classes of priests, soldiers, merchants, laborers, and slaves, ruled by an all-powerful emperor. The Aztecs'

Many Aztec artifacts depict mythical creatures. This two-headed snake is made of wood and covered in turquoise and shells.

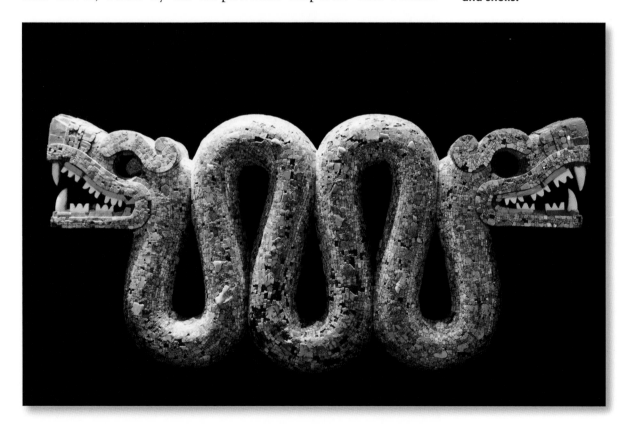

advanced understanding of architecture and mathematics allowed them to construct great pyramids and temples without the use of metal tools or the wheel.

The Spanish Arrive

In 1519, about six hundred Spanish soldiers arrived by ship on the Gulf Coast at the site of what is now the city of Veracruz. By that time, Spain had already established several colonies in North America. Led by Hernán Cortés, the soldiers came in search of an empire rumored to have great wealth.

Hernán Cortés first traveled to the Americas as a teenager. He spent most of the rest of his life there, leading Spain's effort to conquer the Aztec Empire.

As they headed inland, they encountered indigenous peoples who were enemies of the Aztecs. The Spaniards recruited and sometimes forced these people to join them. Armed with cannons, the Spaniards led a force that invaded Tenochtitlán and took the Aztec emperor, Montezuma II, captive. Because of their weapons and the spread of diseases, the Spaniards were able to conquer the Aztecs within two years. Several European diseases such as smallpox were new to the indigenous peoples of the Americas. Huge numbers of indigenous people died from being exposed to them. This helped the Spaniards gain control of the Aztec Empire.

With the defeat of the Aztecs, the area surrounding what is now Mexico City became part of New Spain, the lands Spain claimed in North America. Over time, the Spanish extended

In 1521, Hernán Cortés led an attack of the Aztec capital of Tenochtitlán, which was built on an island that was reached via land bridges.

their control into southern Mexico and eventually came to claim lands in northern Mexico and what is now the western United States.

Life in New Spain

For the indigenous population, life in New Spain was grim. The people who survived the spread of European diseases were forced to work within a labor system called *encomienda*. Under this system, Spain gave Spanish soldiers plots of land to be worked by the indigenous people, with all the products and profits from the farms and mines going to the Spanish, not the laborers.

The Spanish used religion to justify their mistreatment of the local people. They tried to convert the indigenous people to their religion, Roman Catholicism. By converting them, the Spanish believed they would save the indigenous peoples' souls, allowing them to enter heaven when they died. Catholic priests had churches built all over Mexico, often at sites that had been sacred to the local people. To further persuade the people of Mexico to accept Catholicism, the priests melded many local religious rites into Catholic rituals. Over time, most of the people of Mexico became Catholics.

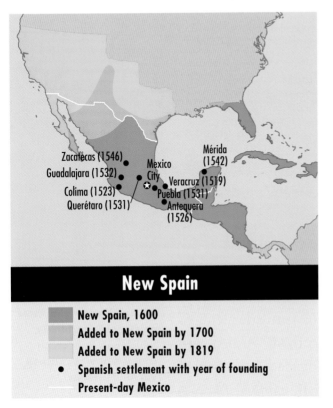

New Spain

New Spain, 1600
Added to New Spain by 1700
Added to New Spain by 1819
• Spanish settlement with year of founding
Present-day Mexico

Zacatecas (1546)
Guadalajara (1532)
Colima (1523)
Querétaro (1531)
Mexico City
Veracruz (1519)
Puebla (1531)
Antequera (1526)
Mérida (1542)

But even after the indigenous people converted, Spaniards still considered them inferior. There developed a strict social ranking system based on people's birthplace, parentage, and skin color. At the top were people born in Spain. Below them were criollos, people of Spanish heritage who were born in Mexico. On the next rung down were mestizos, who had mixed Spanish and indigenous ancestry. At the bottom were people of full indigenous background and a small number of Africans who had been brought to Mexico as slaves.

The War for Independence

As time passed, the criollos became frustrated. Many were wealthy landowners and merchants, but they had little political power. Only people born in Spain could hold high office. The criollos were also angry that Spain seized the minerals and other wealth produced in their own land.

In 1808, France invaded Spain, and the Spanish king was forced from his throne. Sensing Spain was weak, the criollos in Mexico began to think they could free themselves from Spanish rule. A criollo priest named Father Miguel Hidalgo y Costilla led the rebellion. On September 16, 1810, at a church in the town of Dolores in central Mexico, he rang a bell and issued his now-famous *grito*, or cry. Yelling out "Long live Mexico!" Hidalgo called for his people to rise up against the Spanish and take control of their own nation.

Mexicans began fighting Spanish troops for their independence. When Spanish soldiers executed Hidalgo, another priest, José María Morelos y Pavón, became the rebellion's leader. He, too, was killed by the Spanish. The bloody war continued for years. Finally, under the leadership of Agustín de Iturbide, the Mexicans wore down the Spanish forces. In 1821, Spain signed the Treaty of Córdoba, which gave Mexico its independence.

Iturbide soon declared himself the emperor of Mexico. But other rebel leaders did not want him to have complete control over the new country. After they fought and defeated Iturbide, Mexico became a republic—a country in which the people, not an emperor or a king, hold the power.

Father Miguel Hidalgo y Costilla, depicted in this statue, is credited with starting Mexico's movement for independence. A few months after his cry for independence, he was captured and executed.

New Enemies

Mexico was finally independent. But Mexicans did not agree on how it should be governed. Over the next forty years, dozens of governments sprang up, and then promptly fell apart. During this time, Antonio López de Santa Anna, a general who helped overthrow Iturbide, emerged as the country's most powerful political and military leader.

Under Santa Anna, Mexico suffered two humiliating military defeats. In 1836, Mexico was forced to surrender its claim on Texas. Texas became an independent nation for nine years before it was annexed by the United States in 1845. A skirmish over the border of Texas led to the Mexican-American War (1846–1848). During the conflict, an American army arrived by sea at the Mexican port of Veracruz. The soldiers then marched into the heart of the country and captured Mexico City. Defeated, Mexico was forced to give the United States a large expanse of its northern lands, amounting to almost half of all its territory. The area included what became the U.S. states of California, Nevada, and Utah, and portions of New Mexico, Arizona, Colorado, and Wyoming.

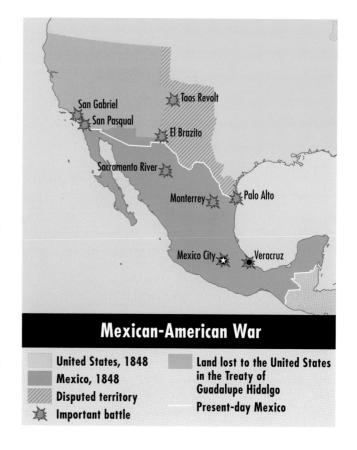

Mexican-American War

United States, 1848
Mexico, 1848
Disputed territory
Important battle
Land lost to the United States in the Treaty of Guadalupe Hidalgo
Present-day Mexico

A LOS DEFENSORES DE LA PATRIA
1846 1847

Los Niños Héroes

On September 13, 1847, thousands of Mexican soldiers stood ready at the Castle of Chapultepec on the western side of Mexico City. They prepared to defend the capital from an American invading force that was fast approaching. Among the Mexicans were cadets from a military academy. About to experience their first taste of battle, most were still in their teens.

The Mexican army failed to repel the American invaders. But even when the battle was lost, six cadets refused to retreat. They chose instead to die fighting. One cadet, Juan Escutia, grabbed the castle's Mexican flag so the Americans could not seize it. Wrapping the flag around his body, he jumped off the castle to his death.

The six cadets are now celebrated as Los Niños Héroes—the child heroes. Every year, on September 13, the Mexican president lays wreaths at a monument at Chapultepec Hill to honor their sacrifice.

A group of liberal reformers pushed Santa Anna out of the presidency in 1854. They wanted to make the Catholic Church and the military less powerful. They also sought to limit the amount of land owned by the church. The reformers drafted a new constitution in 1857. Among other provisions, it guaranteed freedom of speech and freedom of the press.

Conservative Mexicans, particularly church officials and members of the military, rejected the constitution. A civil war broke out. After four years of fighting, the liberal faction won. Its exiled leader, Benito Juárez, returned to Mexico City to serve as president.

Santa Anna's Lost Leg

Mexican general and president Santa Anna was unlucky enough to lose a leg in battle—not once, but twice.

In 1838, Santa Anna was fighting French troops at Veracruz when a cannonball splintered his ankle. His doctor had to amputate most of the leg. Santa Anna buried the leg at Veracruz, but four years later, as president, he had it dug up. The leg was transported in a decorated coach to Mexico City. There it was reburied with full military honors.

After his leg was amputated, Santa Anna began wearing an artificial leg made of wood and cork. During the Mexican-American War, he had to leave the artificial leg behind when his army made a hasty retreat after the Battle of Cerro Gordo. American soldiers from Illinois found the leg in his carriage and took it home. It was displayed at county fairs before finding its permanent home at the Illinois State Military Museum.

The French Take Control

The war had bankrupted Mexico. It owed money to Spain, Great Britain, and France. Troops from those countries landed at Veracruz to pressure Mexico to pay its debts. The Spanish and British soon left, but the French soldiers moved toward Mexico City. They were supported by Mexican conservative leaders. The French seized the capital, and Benito Juárez fled the country. In 1863, the French named Ferdinand Maximilian, the archduke of Austria, the new emperor of Mexico.

His rule was short. Maximilian took land from the Church, so the conservatives abandoned him. France withdrew its troops because they were needed back home. Juárez's supporters reclaimed Mexico City and executed Maximilian. Juárez assumed the presidency and worked to reform Mexico's economy until his death in 1872.

The Porfiriato

A few years later, Porfirio Díaz rose to power. He was Mexico's president for most years between 1876 and 1910. This period

3 1613 00515 5067

CALUMET CITY
PUBLIC LIBRARY

A Beloved President

One of the most beloved statesmen in Mexican history, Benito Júarez served as the president from 1858 to 1872.

Júarez was born in 1806 in a small farming village to poor parents. He and his family were Zapotec Indians. While still a boy, Júarez left home for the city of Oaxaca to go to school.

Júarez became a lawyer and a judge. He also entered politics. Beginning in 1847, Júarez served as the governor of the state of Oaxaca for five years. He worked to improve roads and schools.

In 1853, Júarez was exiled from Mexico by President Santa Anna, who considered him a political enemy. He returned when Santa Anna was forced from power. He then served in the president's cabinet and on the Supreme Court.

In the late 1850s and early 1860s, Mexico was plunged into turmoil. It suffered first a civil war and then a takeover of the government by French soldiers. During this time, liberals claimed Júarez was the country's rightful president.

After the French-controlled government was toppled in 1867, Júarez assumed the presidency. He worked to

strengthen the economy, build railroads, and increase access to education. But his efforts were often blocked by his conservative political opponents. Júarez's presidency came to a sudden end in 1872 when he died of a heart attack. He is still admired as a fair and honest politician who devoted his life to helping his people.

in the history of Mexico is now called the Porfiriato.

Like Juárez, Díaz started his political career as a liberal. With the help of U.S. investors, he worked to modernize Mexico by building railroads and telephone lines. But he soon started to rule as a dictator, ignoring the will of the people. Díaz continued to win the presidency only because he rigged the elections. During the Porfiriato, Mexico's rich became richer, while poor workers lost land and saw their incomes shrink.

Many Mexicans were angered by Díaz's stranglehold on political power. One such opponent was Francisco Madero. He ran against Díaz in the 1910 presidential election. Just before the vote, Díaz threw Madero in jail and declared himself the winner. Madero escaped to Texas and called for his fellow Mexicans to take up arms against the government. On November 20, 1910, the Mexican Revolution began.

The Mexican Revolution

Rebel leaders, including Pancho Villa in the north and Emiliano Zapata in the south, responded to Madero's call for

Poor Mexican workers carry bundles of wood on their backs in the early twentieth century.

Pancho Villa (front, center) meets with Emiliano Zapata (front, right) in Mexico City in 1915, in the midst of the Mexican Revolution.

revolution. Díaz was forced to resign, and Madero returned to Mexico, winning the presidency in 1911. But from the beginning, conservatives opposed his rule. Madero was arrested and executed, and military leader Victoriano Huerta took power.

Villa joined with two allies, Álvaro Obregón and Venustiano Carranza, to fight Huerta. They forced him out of office. But then Carranza declared himself president, which angered Villa. Mexico fell into chaos as Villa, Obregón, and Zapata began fighting Carranza.

Soon, Obregón shifted his allegiance back to Carranza, and the more radical Villa and Zapata were pushed to the margins. Carranza also had the support of the U.S. government, which sent troops over the border to fight Villa's men. Villa and Zapata were later assassinated, but both are now revered as folk heroes in Mexico because they fought for the interests of the poor and the landless.

Mexico adopted a new constitution in 1917. It instituted many liberal reforms. For instance, it strengthened workers' rights and shifted control over schools to the government and away from the Church. But the fighting between various groups continued for years. The Mexican Revolution took a terrible toll on the Mexican people. About 10 percent of the population died during the war and thousands fled the country, many to the United States.

The Rise of the PRI

By the late 1920s, Mexico became more politically stable. At that time, the country's major political party, now called the Institutional Revolutionary Party (known as the PRI, its initials in Spanish), was founded. For about seventy years, the leaders of the PRI controlled every aspect of Mexico's government.

At first, the PRI tried to make many changes the revolution's supporters had demanded. For instance, President Lázaro Cárdenas, who served from 1934 to 1940, tried to help workers form unions and give poor people access to land and schools. Under his leadership, the Mexican government took control of the country's oil resources, which had been managed by American companies.

After World War II (1939–1945), Mexico's economy grew quickly. The government built roads and factories. Many workers moved from rural areas to cities, where they could find better-paying jobs. For the first time, some Mexicans who had grown up in poverty could earn a good living. But many people remained poor.

The PRI wanted industries to grow and businesspeople to prosper. But it became less concerned about Mexican workers who were left behind. The PRI began to rig elections to stay in power. It also intimidated anyone who opposed the party. Many reporters feared they would be punished if they criticized the PRI in any way.

Political Troubles

But not everyone stayed silent. In 1968, a group of students staged a protest against the government in Mexico City. The army and police opened fire into the crowd. At least forty protesters were killed, but some reports said there were hundreds of casualties. The violent response angered the Mexican people. Many lost all confidence in the PRI.

National Palace

In the center of Mexico City stands the Palacio Nacional, or National Palace. When Mexico was part of New Spain, the majestic building was the home of the viceroy, the head of the Spanish-controlled government.

Today, the National Palace contains government offices, as well as some of Mexico's most famous works of art. For more than twenty years, the painter Diego Rivera covered vast stretches of wall space with colorful murals. Rivera's works illustrate Mexican history. They include paintings of the ancient civilizations, including the Aztecs, the Spanish conquest of Mexico, and the Mexican fight for independence. Other notable features of the National Palace are a museum devoted to Mexican president Benito Juárez and a great fountain with a statue of Pegasus, a mythical winged horse.

Zapatista rebels rally in Mexico City in the 1990s. The Zapatistas fought for the rights of indigenous people and for local control of the natural resources in their home state of Chiapas.

Even more people became fed up with the government in 1985, when Mexico City suffered a massive earthquake. About ten thousand people died, and some three hundred thousand lost their homes. The government was slow to respond to the crisis. Earthquake victims never received much of the money foreign countries contributed to help them.

In 1994, Mexico faced several crises. In January, a revolutionary group in the southern state of Chiapas staged an uprising in response to the start of the North American Free Trade Agreement (NAFTA), which eliminated taxes on many goods shipped between Mexico and the United States. The rebels, mostly Maya people, called themselves the Zapatista Army of National Liberation and challenged the government's participation in NAFTA. They claimed that the government, the wealthy, and business interests were ignoring the needs of the poor and landless. In March, PRI presidential candidate Luis Donaldo Colosio was assassinated. And in December, a national financial crisis left many workers without jobs. The United States had to give Mexico billions of dollars to keep the economy from collapsing, ensuring the continued strength of NAFTA.

The widespread disappointment with the PRI led to changes in Mexico's political system. Elections became more closely monitored, and other political parties found more supporters. In 2000, the PRI's hold on the Mexican presidency was broken with the election of Vicente Fox. Fox was a member of the National Action Party, known as PAN after its initials in Spanish.

Fighting the Drug Trade

Another problem facing modern Mexico is drug trafficking. Heavily armed cartels transport illegal drugs from South America through Mexico and into the United States. Cartels are organizations of people that supply and smuggle illegal drugs and weapons. Innocent people are often killed in wars between rival cartels. Drug traffickers also threaten and sometimes murder elected officials and journalists who speak out against them.

Taking on the drug trade was a focus of the administration of Felipe Calderón, who became president in 2006. Calderón dispatched about fifty thousand troops to battle Mexico's drug cartels. The troops, however, only made the drug-related violence worse. During Calderón's six-year presidency, sixty thousand people were murdered.

Drug violence continued to be a major issue for the next president, Enrique Peña Nieto. Since his election in 2012, he has been criticized for his failure to deal with the problem. The public became particularly outraged after the abduction of forty-three male college students in 2014. The government said that drug cartels were responsible. But an independent investigation poked holes in the government's account. It did not solve the mystery of what happened to the students, but it did suggest that the government was trying to cover up the army's involvement in the disappearances. In September 2016, thousands of protesters took to the streets in Mexico City to demand answers.

Despite the violence, Mexico is thriving in many ways. Its economy has grown steadily in recent years, and many more people are moving into the middle class.

Demonstrators fill the streets of Mexico City on the second anniversary of the disappearance of forty-three college students. The protesters were demanding that the government find out what happened to the students.

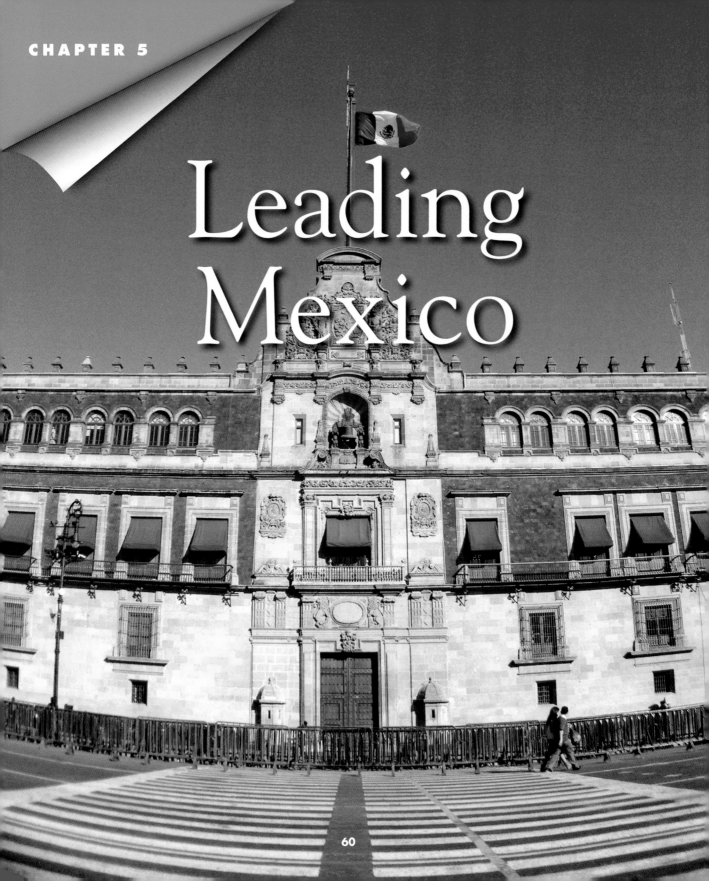

CHAPTER 5

Leading Mexico

MEXICO IS MADE UP OF THIRTY-ONE STATES and the Federal District, which encompasses Mexico City, the nation's capital. The federal, or national, government of Mexico is based in the Federal District.

Mexico's government operates under rules set out in the Constitution of 1917. This document established the country's three branches of government—the executive, the legislative, and the judicial.

Opposite: **The site of the National Palace has a long history in Mexico. An Aztec palace once stood there. After the National Palace was built, many Spanish viceroys lived there, as did the early presidents of Mexico. Today, the building houses some government offices.**

Mexico's National Government

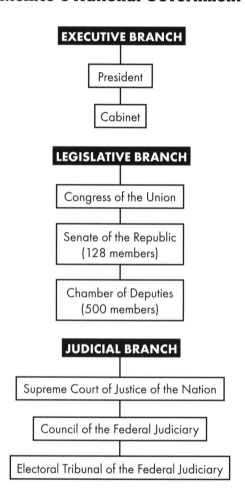

EXECUTIVE BRANCH

President

Cabinet

LEGISLATIVE BRANCH

Congress of the Union

Senate of the Republic
(128 members)

Chamber of Deputies
(500 members)

JUDICIAL BRANCH

Supreme Court of Justice of the Nation

Council of the Federal Judiciary

Electoral Tribunal of the Federal Judiciary

Heading the Government

The president is the head of the executive branch. He or she is elected directly by voters. Anyone eighteen or older is eligible to vote. Voting is compulsory, which means that every eligible voter is required by law to cast a ballot. But in practice no one is punished for not voting.

The president serves a term of six years. Once the term is over, he or she can never run for president again. The rule is in place to prevent any one person from gaining control over the government for a long period of time. But the president, while in office, is very powerful. The president is head of state, head of the government, and the commander in chief of the armed forces.

A woman in Mexico City casts her ballots. Each box is for a different office. For example, one is for the president, and another is for the head of the government in Mexico City.

The president is responsible for selecting the cabinet. The cabinet includes eighteen secretaries, each in charge of a particular part of the Mexican government. For example, there are secretaries for foreign affairs, labor, energy, communications, education, and tourism. If the president is dissatisfied with a secretary, he or she is free to fire the secretary and appoint a new one.

The president also selects the head of the Bank of Mexico and the attorney general, who advises the government about

Members of Mexico's Chamber of Deputies raise their hands to vote on a bill.

legal matters. These candidates must be approved by Mexico's Senate.

Making Laws

The legislative branch of the Mexican government is in charge of making laws. Mexico's national legislative body is the Congress of the Union. It has two houses, the Senate of the Republic and the Chamber of Deputies.

The Senate has 128 members. The Chamber of Deputies has five hundred seats. Senators are elected for six years; deputies, for three. Until recently, senators and deputies were not allowed to serve two terms in a row. But many Mexicans complained that lawmakers did not feel they had to make good on their campaign promises because they did not have to worry about reelection. Responding to these concerns, President Enrique Peña Nieto changed the rules in 2014. Now senators

A Look at the Capital

The ancient Aztecs believed their capital, Tenochtitlán, stood at the center of the world. Tenochtitlán was leveled by the Spanish, who then built on its ruins another great urban center—the Mexican capital of Mexico City.

Mexico City is in the Valley of Mexico, known to the Aztecs as Anahuac. Surrounded by mountains, it rests on a high plateau. The city center is about 7,350 feet (2,240 m) above sea level.

Mexico City itself has a population of about 8.9 million, but about 21 million people live in the city and its surrounding metropolitan area. It is the country's greatest economic and cultural center. Gleaming skyscrapers line the Paseo de la Reforma (above right). Mexico City's landmarks include the Torre Latinoamericana (Latin American Tower); the Metropolitan Cathedral (below right), a Catholic church from the city's Spanish

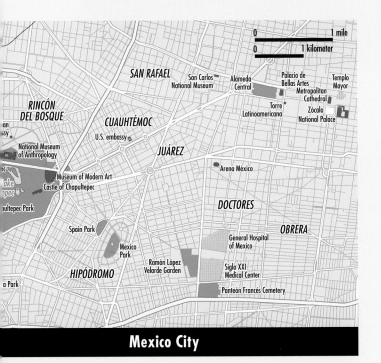

Mexico City

era; and Templo Mayor, an excavated Aztec pyramid. Mexico City is also known for a large plaza called the Zócalo, one of the largest city squares in the world.

Mexico City faces some challenging problems common to large urban centers around the world. Many of its residents are poor. The crime rate is high. Its air is polluted, and its roads are clogged with traffic. But still, about one thousand Mexicans move to the city from other areas every day. These newcomers are looking for the opportunities and excitement that they can only find in their great and growing capital.

EL RESPETO AL
DERECHO AJENO
ES LA PAZ

Justices on the Supreme Court of Justice hear a case.

can serve two consecutive six-year terms, and deputies four three-year terms.

In addition to making laws, the Congress can levy taxes, declare war, and approve treaties and budgets. Because Mexico has no vice president, Congress also has the responsibility of appointing a replacement for the president if he or she dies or resigns.

Serving Justice

The third branch of federal government is the judicial system. The Supreme Court is the highest court in the land. It

The Mexican Flag

The flag of Mexico features three vertical bands—one green, one white, and one red. The green represents

hope, white stands for purity, and red for the color of the blood of those who fought for Mexico's independence from Spain in the early nineteenth century.

In the middle of the flag's white band is a picture of a golden eagle perched on a cactus. The eagle is devouring a rattlesnake with its beak. The image is inspired by an Aztec legend: The Aztecs were once wandering in search of the perfect place to build a settlement. Their god told them to look for an eagle eating a snake while resting on a cactus. The Aztecs finally spied the eagle at the site of what is now Mexico City. There, they built the great city of Tenochtitlán, the capital of the Aztec Empire.

can strike down a law if the law is at odds with the Mexican constitution.

The Supreme Court is composed of eleven justices. They choose one of their members to serve as chief justice. The chief justice holds this post for four years.

All Supreme Court justices are appointed by the president. However, before taking the bench, nominees must first be approved by two-thirds of all senators. Justices serve a fifteen-year term and cannot be reappointed.

The judicial branch also includes district and circuit courts. Judges in these lower courts are appointed by the Council of the Federal Judiciary. Another important body in the national judicial system is the Electoral Tribunal. It resolves any disputes regarding fraud or other problems with federal elections.

Supporters of the PRI attend a rally. The party has dominated Mexican politics for most of the last century.

State and Local Governments

Mexico's thirty-one states each have their own constitutions and governments. The head of each state's executive branch is the governor. This leader serves for six years and cannot be reelected.

State laws are made by state legislatures. Their members are elected to three-year terms and meet twice a year. In each state, the governor nominates and the legislature approves the justices of the state's Superior Court. These justices are responsible for appointing all judges on lower courts within the state.

Mexico is also divided into about 2,400 municipalities. Municipalities are similar to counties in the United States. They are led by a mayor and a council. Governors often have a hand in choosing who runs in municipal elections. The budget of a municipality also has to be approved by the governor. State and local governments raise little money themselves. They rely heavily on funds given to them by the federal government.

Political Parties

Mexico has many political parties. But until recently one had almost exclusive control over the government at all levels. The powerful Institutional Revolutionary Party (PRI) held the presidency and the majority in both houses of the Congress from 1929 to 1997.

However, in the twenty-first century, two other political parties have become more prominent in national elections. The National Action Party (PAN) is more conservative than the PRI. It is favored by many businesspeople and the Catholic Church. The Party of the Democratic Revolution (PRD) is more liberal. It supports more government programs that help workers and the poor.

In 2000, Mexico elected Vicente Fox president. A member of PAN, he was the first modern president who was not a member of the PRI. PAN retained the presidency in 2006, when Felipe Calderón was elected. But six years later, PRI won back the presidency with the election of Enrique Peña Nieto.

Ending Corruption

Peña Nieto has struggled in office. Critics complain that he does not have the political talent needed to get things done. Peña Nieto is also very unpopular because he has done little to solve one of the Mexican government's greatest problems—corruption.

Corrupt government officials take money and gifts in exchange for favors. Peña Nieto himself has been caught up in several corruption scandals. In the eyes of many Mexicans, police and government corruption is a national crisis. They are convinced that problems such as poverty and violent crime will never be solved until the government takes corruption more seriously. Many citizens have become activists. They are demanding reforms in the government to put an end to corruption once and for all.

A protester holds up a sign in opposition to Enrique Peña Nieto, the leader of the PRI.

"Mexicans, to the War Cry"

In 1853, President Antonio López de Santa Anna was very unpopular with the Mexican people. He decided to rally their support by holding a contest to create a new patriotic anthem. Mexicans were invited to submit lyrics.

The poet Francisco González Bocanegra considered entering the contest. But when he sat down to write, he felt uninspired. Legend holds that his girlfriend locked him in a room and told him he could not come out until he had finished his submission. Four hours later, he slipped his lyrics under the door.

Bocanegra's entry won. His lyrics were later put to music by Spanish-born composer Jaime Nunó Roca. The official name of the song is "Himno Nacional Mexicano" ("National Anthem of Mexico"), but its informal title comes from its first line: "Mexicans, to the War Cry." The anthem celebrates Mexicans' determination to defend their beloved homeland.

Spanish lyrics	English translation
Mexicanos, al grito de guerra	Mexicans, to the war cry,
El acero aprestad y el bridón,	Prepare the steel and the bridle,
y retiemble en sus centros la tierra	And shake the earth to its core
Al sonoro rugir del cañón.	By the roar of the cannon.
Ciña ¡oh patria! tus sienes de oliva	Gird, oh country, your brow with the olive wreath
De la paz el arcángel divino,	Of the divine archangel of peace,
Que en el cielo tu eterno destino	For in heaven your eternal destiny
Por el dedo de Dios se escribió.	Was written by the finger of God.
Más si osare un extraño enemigo	But should a foreign enemy dare
Profanar con su planta tu suelo,	Dishonor your ground with his sole,
Piensa ¡oh patria querida! que el cielo	Recall, beloved fatherland, that heaven
Un soldado en cada hijo te dio.	Gave you a soldier in each son.

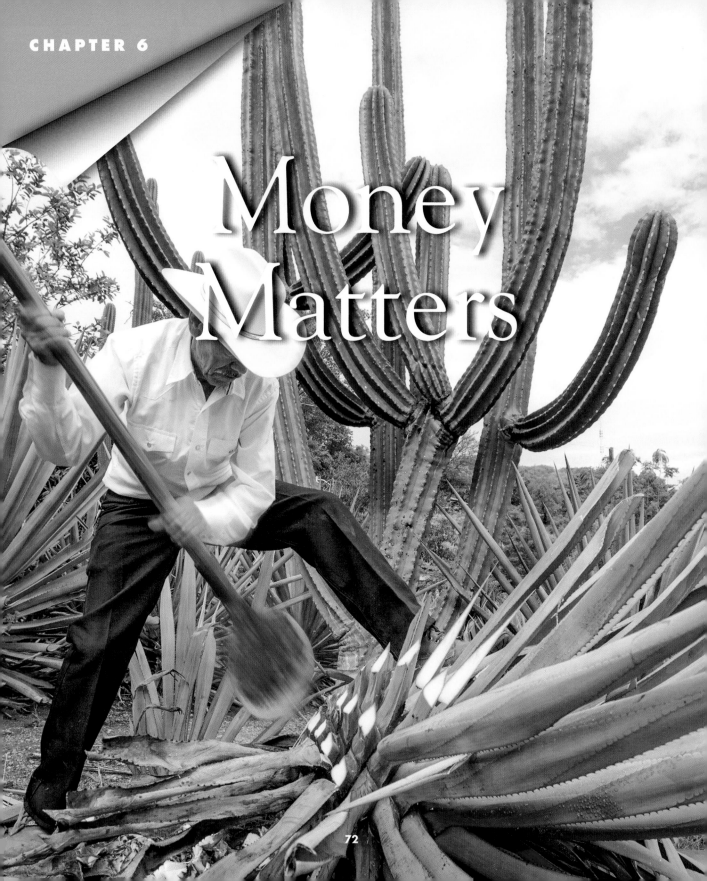

CHAPTER 6

Money Matters

NOT TOO LONG AGO, MOST MEXICANS WERE FARMERS. But in the late 1940s, Mexico began to modernize its economy. It built new roads and promoted new businesses. Many Mexicans responded by moving from the countryside to cities. There, they could find jobs in factories and offices. In urban areas, they also had better access to food, decent housing, and health care.

In just a few decades, Mexico experienced tremendous economic growth. Today, its economy is the fifteenth largest in the world. It is now home to skyscrapers, highways, airports, and power plants.

But not everyone has reaped the benefits of this progress. Some people have thrived. Many more are struggling. In the twenty-first century, Mexico is looking to make the most of its resources, while improving the economic lot of all its people.

Opposite: **A farmer harvests a blue agave cactus. The cactus provides an important ingredient in the popular alcoholic drink tequila.**

A worker walks across a vast storage facility in southeastern Mexico. The facility can hold a half a million barrels of oil.

Minerals and Oil

Mexico is rich in minerals. It produces more silver than any other country in the world. Mexico also has large deposits of copper, gold, lead, zinc, iron, and manganese.

Even more important to Mexico's economy is its oil reserves. It is one of the world's largest oil producers. Every day, Mexico produces about 2.2 million barrels of crude oil.

The oil industry is controlled by Petróleos Mexicanos, or Pemex. The company, formed in 1938, is owned by the national government. About one-third of all government revenue comes from selling oil. In recent decades, Mexico has struggled to find the funds to increase its oil income. Since 2014, the country has been looking to foreign investors for the money needed to discover and drill new oil fields.

Farming, Fishing, and Forestry

Until recently, farming was a central part of Mexico's economy. But now only about 13 percent of its people work in agriculture. Some families in central and southern Mexico still operate small farms, growing mostly native corn and beans. The most productive farms, however, are located in the north. The large agricultural businesses there are run by corporations. Using modern technology to cultivate irrigated land, these farms grow melons, strawberries, cucumbers, tomatoes, coffee, and cotton. Most of their harvested crops are exported for sale in the United States.

Some Mexicans make their living in the fishing industry. In the Pacific Ocean off western Mexico, fishers catch lobster, albacore, and anchovies. In the Gulf of Mexico in the east,

"Butterfly fishermen" work on Lake Pátzcuaro in Michoacán, a state in western Mexico. They catch fish using traditional butterfly-shaped nets.

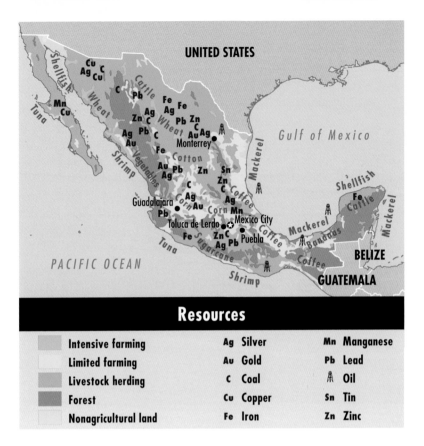

Resources

Intensive farming	Ag	Silver	Mn Manganese
Limited farming	Au	Gold	Pb Lead
Livestock herding	C	Coal	Oil
Forest	Cu	Copper	Sn Tin
Nonagricultural land	Fe	Iron	Zn Zinc

they find snapper, mackerel, and croaker. Shrimp is an important fishing product on both coasts.

Forests cover about one-third of Mexico. In central Mexico, pines and oaks grow on mountain slopes. The southeast has forests of mahogany and other tropical trees. The forestry industry of Mexico produces wood used for building construction and fuel. But it has been criticized in recent years for overlogging, threatening Mexico's forests.

Services and Manufacturing

The majority of Mexican workers—a full two-thirds—are part of the service industry. Service jobs are found in education, banking, medicine, and other fields. Many service workers are employed in tourism. They include tour guides, restaurant workers, cruise ship personnel, and hotel employees. Mexico welcomes more than twenty million international tourists a year. Most are from the United States and Canada.

About one-fourth of Mexican jobs are in manufacturing. Products made in Mexico include processed foods, beverages,

Workers at a plant in northern Mexico construct jet airplane parts for an American company.

clothing, chemicals, plastics, paper products, machinery, and vehicles.

Many Mexicans work in *maquiladoras*, or foreign-owned factories. These factories are located near the border with the United States. American companies send parts to maquiladoras, where Mexican laborers assemble the parts into products, such as cars and machinery. Once assembled, the products are then sold in the United States. This system, which began in the 1960s, is profitable for American companies because Mexican workers are paid less than American workers. In recent years, though, companies have started to relocate assembly plants to Asia, where labor costs are even lower.

Mexican manufacturing had been boosted by the North American Free Trade Agreement (NAFTA). This agreement encouraged trade between Mexico, the United States, and Canada. It also allowed for more foreigners to invest in Mexican businesses. By making it easy to export goods to its northern neighbors, NAFTA greatly increased the market for goods made in Mexico. But many small family-owned farms in Mexico, especially those that grew native corn varieties, were devastated by NAFTA.

The United States is now Mexico's most important trading partner. About 90 percent of products exported by Mexico are sold to Americans. China and Japan also import Mexican-made goods such as machinery, electrical equipment, and automobile parts.

What Mexico Grows, Makes, and Mines

AGRICULTURE (2014)

Corn	23,400,000 metric tons
Tomatoes	2,900,000 metric tons
Avocados	1,520,000 metric tons

MANUFACTURING

Automobiles (2014)	3,200,000 units
Shoes (2012)	250,000 pairs
Soft drinks (2014)	28,141,000,000 plastic and glass bottles

MINING

Oil (2016)	2,193,000 barrels per day
Copper (2013)	409,172 metric tons
Silver (2013)	5,821 metric tons

Working in the United States

Mexico not only exports goods to the United States; it also exports workers. Many Mexicans, particularly young men, travel across the border looking for jobs.

For many workers, a job in the United States pays more than a job in Mexico. Often, they can make enough to send some money home to their families. Money sent home to relatives is called a remittance. This money can make a great difference to Mexicans, who might go hungry or might not be able to afford an education without it.

Many Mexican workers enter the United States legally, with the proper documents. But others sneak across the border to fill poor-paying jobs. These undocumented workers have caused tensions between the United States and Mexico. Some Americans believe these workers cause lower wages and take jobs away from Americans.

Mexico has its own problem with undocumented immigration. Impoverished people and refugees from Guatemala and

Mexican immigrants work in a tulip field in Washington State. Most agricultural workers in the United States are immigrants.

other Central American countries often cross the border into Mexico in search of a better life. Some travel through Mexico to get to the United States.

The Wealth Gap

Many workers who stay in Mexico often find it hard to get by. Many cannot find regular jobs with benefits. The only work they can get is irregular and unpredictable. As many as 65 percent of Mexican workers are employed in this unregulated,

An elderly woman sells onions and tomatoes at an outdoor market.

Money Facts

The basic unit of currency in Mexico is the peso. In 2017, US$1 was worth about 21 Mexican pesos.

In Mexico, banknotes come in values of 20, 50, 100, 200, 500, and 1,000 pesos. There are also 5, 10, and 20 peso coins.

Most of the banknotes feature portraits of important historical figures on the front and images of famous landmarks and buildings on the back. The 500-peso bill, however, pays tribute to two of Mexico's best-known artists. Muralist Diego Rivera appears on the front, and painter Frida Kahlo is pictured on the back.

informal economy. They often earn the equivalent of only a few dollars a day.

Addressing poverty is one of Mexico's greatest challenges. About 52 percent of the population is poor. Poverty is particularly widespread in rural areas. Day to day, some people cannot be sure of getting enough food to eat.

Many Mexicans who live in cities are middle class. But in the countryside, people tend to be either poor or rich, with very few in between. The rich in Mexico are small in number, but they possess an enormous amount of money. The richest 10 percent of the Mexican population owns 60 percent of the country's wealth.

This great gap between the rich and poor has long been a problem. Some Mexicans are resigned that nothing will ever change. But others are speaking out against what they see as an unfair economic system. They are calling on their government to do more to create good jobs and help the poor.

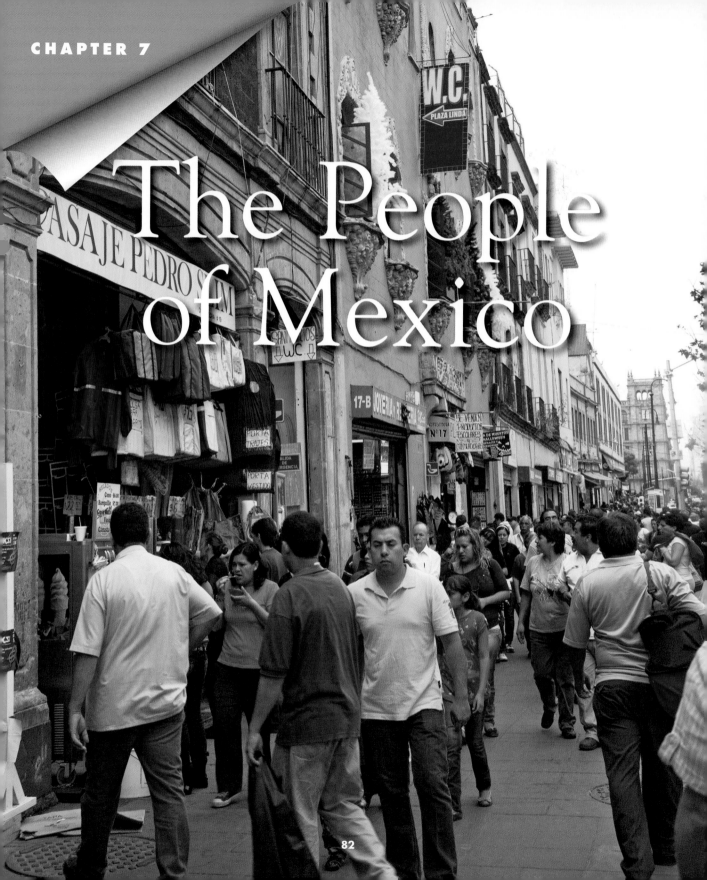

CHAPTER 7

The People of Mexico

MEXICO IS HOME TO ABOUT 123 MILLION PEOPLE. The country's population is the twelfth largest in the world.

Mexico's population is fairly young. More than one-quarter of Mexicans are fourteen years old or younger. Nearly half are under twenty-four. Only about 7 percent of its people are over sixty-five.

Most Mexicans live in the central portion of the country. About one person in six is a resident of the metropolitan area around the capital of Mexico City. The Mexican population as a whole is very urbanized. Almost 80 percent of the population lives in cities. In 2010, ten Mexican cities had a population greater than one million.

Opposite: **Pedestrians crowd the sidewalks of a shopping district in Mexico City. Mexico City is the center of one of the largest urban areas in the world.**

A Maya girl walks with relatives at a festival in Chiapas.

Ethnic Identity

About 30 percent of Mexicans are mostly or fully descended from the indigenous peoples who lived in Mexico before the arrival of the Spanish. There are about sixty Indian groups in Mexico today. Each has its own language, customs, and beliefs. The southern states of Guerrero, Oaxaca, and Chiapas have the greatest Indian populations.

The largest Mexican Indian group is the Nahuas, who number about three million. They claim the Aztecs as their ancestors. Some two million Mayas now live in the Yucatán Peninsula. Other large Indian groups include the Zapotecs, Tzotziles, Tzeltales, Mixtecs, Otomis, and Totonacs.

Another 10 percent of Mexicans are of European, Asian, or African heritage. But the majority of Mexicans—about 60 per-

Afro-Mexicans

Until recently, one ethnic minority was all but invisible to the Mexican government. That changed in 2016 when the country's census bureau conducted a survey to determine how many Afro-Mexicans—Mexicans of African descent—lived within its borders. The survey found almost 1.4 million Afro-Mexican citizens, making up about 1.2 percent of the total Mexican population.

Beginning in the sixteenth century, Spaniards brought enslaved Africans to Mexico. They were brought in to replace Indian workers who had died from diseases. Slavery was abolished in 1829, but the slaves' descen-dants remained in Mexico. Today, Afro-Mexicans are clustered primarily in two areas—around the city of Veracruz on the Gulf of Mexico and in the southwestern states of Guerrero and Oaxaca on the Pacific coast.

Afro-Mexicans are asking the government for more say in policy decisions affecting them. One group, México Negro, is also seeking changes in history books used in Mexican schools. The books already detail the roles played by Indian and Spanish people in shaping Mexico. The activists want Afro-Mexicans to also be acknowledged for their part in the nation's history.

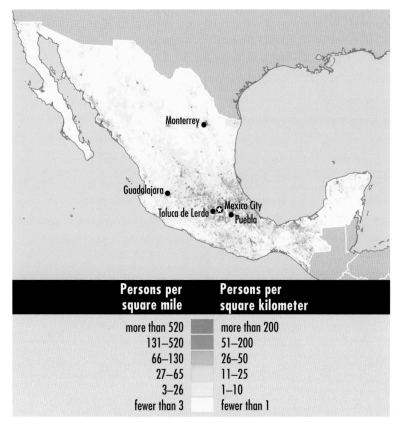

Persons per square mile		Persons per square kilometer	
more than 520		more than 200	
131–520		51–200	
66–130		26–50	
27–65		11–25	
3–26		1–10	
fewer than 3		fewer than 1	

Ethnic Groups in Mexico

Mestizo (mixed Spanish-indigenous ancestry)	62%
Mostly indigenous	21%
Fully indigenous	7%
Afro-Mexican	1%
Other (mostly European)	9%

cent—identify themselves as mestizos, or people of Indian and Spanish ancestry. Mexico has long been proud of its mixed population. When European explorers and settlers arrived in Mexico, they often fought with Indian peoples, and the Spanish often treated the indigenous people cruelly. However, over time, the two groups found a way to live together, resulting in a largely mestizo population.

Race and Society

Mexicans like to think that they do not have the racial inequality seen in the United States. But in some ways, mestizos and Indians are treated differently in Mexican society. Mestizos are more likely to live in cities, hold better jobs, and have college degrees. Many Indians live in poor rural communities. They have less access to education and political power.

Regardless of their actual ancestry, people with darker skin are sometimes discriminated against. Light skin is also linked to higher social status. People appearing on television or in advertising, for instance, usually have a light complexion.

Speaking Spanish and English

Regardless of their background, nearly all Mexicans speak Spanish. In fact, there are more Spanish speakers in Mexico than in any other country, including Spain. Spanish is the first language of about 93 percent of the population. Another 6 percent know how to speak both Spanish and an Indian language.

The Spanish spoken in Mexico is slightly different from the Spanish spoken in Spain. Some sounds are pronounced differently, and each country has its own slang. But just as an American can understand a British person's English, a Mexican can understand a Spaniard's Spanish.

In almost all schools, classes are taught in Spanish. Children are required to attend preschool and six years of both primary and secondary school. Studying English is mandatory in upper grades, but some students begin learning the language as soon as they start school. Knowledge of English is needed in many lines of work because Mexico does so much business

Common Spanish Words and Phrases

¡Hola!	Hello
Adiós	Good-bye
Buenos días	Good morning
Buenas noches	Good night
Sí	Yes
No	No
¿Qué tal?	How is it going?/How are you?
Por favor	Please
Gracias	Thank you
De nada	You're welcome

Many schools in Mexico require students to wear uniforms.

with the United States. It is especially helpful in the tourism industry because so many Americans travel to Mexico on vacation.

Indian Languages

A small minority of Mexicans do not know Spanish or English. Less than 1 percent of the population speaks only one of about 143 indigenous languages still heard in Mexico. These languages include Nahuatl, Maya, Zapotec, Mixtec, Otomi, Tzeltal, Tzotzil, and others. Many people who know only an Indian language live in isolated communities. They rarely interact with anyone outside their Indian group.

In recent decades, many people from the countryside have moved to cities to find work. To succeed, they have had to learn at least some Spanish. Often, though, urban Indians want to learn Spanish well because it helps them find better opportunities in Mexican society. They sometimes stop speaking their first language altogether.

Because fewer Mexicans are speaking Indian languages, some of these languages may soon completely disappear. Experts fear that about twenty-one are endangered. Ayapenaco, for instance, is spoken by only a handful of people, most of whom are elderly. In a few years, there may no longer be any speakers of Ayapenaco alive.

Today, scholars are working to document these languages. They are recording the native speakers of these languages in an effort to preserve this vital part of Mexico's cultural heritage.

A sign at Mitla, a Zapotec site in Oaxaca, describes a historic building in three languages: Spanish, Zapotec, and English.

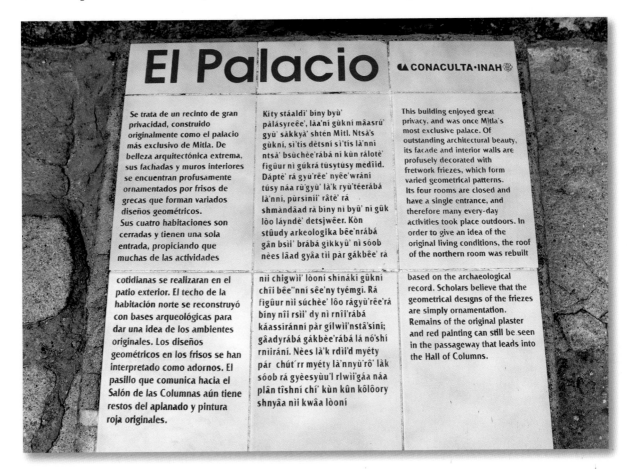

El Palacio

▲CONACULTA·INAH

Se trata de un recinto de gran privacidad, construido originalmente como el palacio más exclusivo de Mitla. De belleza arquitectónica extrema, sus fachadas y muros interiores se encuentran profusamente ornamentados por frisos de grecas que forman variados diseños geométricos. Sus cuatro habitaciones son cerradas y tienen una sola entrada, propiciando que muchas de las actividades cotidianas se realizaran en el patio exterior. El techo de la habitación norte se reconstruyó con bases arqueológicas para dar una idea de los ambientes originales. Los diseños geométricos en los frisos se han interpretado como adornos. El pasillo que comunica hacia el Salón de las Columnas aún tiene restos del aplanado y pintura roja originales.

Kíty stáaldi' biny byù' pàlásyreêe', làa'ni gùkni mâasrú' gyù' sàkkyà' shtén Mitl. Ntsà's gùkni, si'tis dètsni si'tis là'nni ntsà' bsùchèe'rábá ní kùn rálotè' fìgûur ni gùkrá túsytúsy medîid. Dápte' rá gyu'rêe' nyêe'wrání túsy nàa rù'gyù' là'k ryù'téerábá là'nni, pùrsinii' râtê' rá shmàndàad rá biny ni byù' ni gùk lòo láyndè' detsjwêer. Kòn stûudy arkeologika bêe'nrábá gân bsii' brábá gikkyù' nì sóob nèes làad gyâa tii pàr gákbêe' rá nii chigwii' lòoni shináki gùkni chîi bêe"nni sêe'ny tyémgi. Rá fìgûur nìi súchèe' lôo rágyù'rêe'rá bíny nîi rsii' dy nì rnîi'rábá kàassiránni pàr gìlwìi'nstâ'síni; gâadyrábá gákbèe'rábá lá nó'shi rniiráni. Nèes là'k rdìi'd myéty pàr chút'rr myéty là'nnyù'rô' làk sóob rá gyèesyùu'l rlwii'gáa náa plàn tîshni chí' kùn kûn kôlôory shnyâa nìi kwâa lòoni

This building enjoyed great privacy, and was once Mitla's most exclusive palace. Of outstanding architectural beauty, its facade and interior walls are profusely decorated with fretwork friezes, which form varied geometrical patterns. Its four rooms are closed and have a single entrance, and therefore many every-day activities took place outdoors. In order to give an idea of the original living conditions, the roof of the northern room was rebuilt based on the archaeological record. Scholars believe that the geometrical designs of the friezes are simply ornamentation. Remains of the original plaster and red painting can still be seen in the passageway that leads into the Hall of Columns.

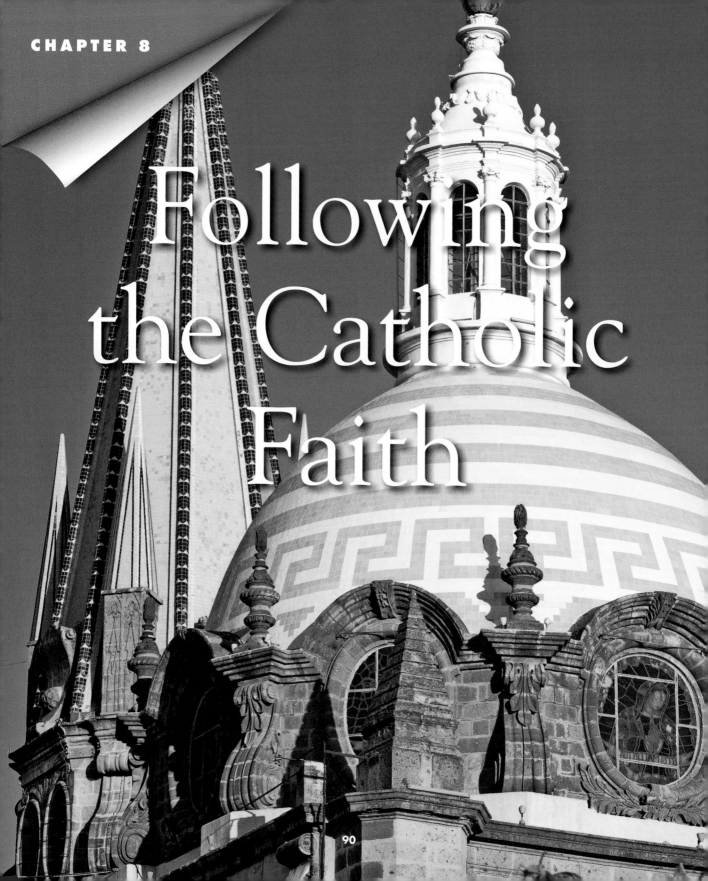

CHAPTER 8

Following the Catholic Faith

W HEN THE SPANISH ARRIVED IN WHAT IS NOW Mexico, they intended to forcibly convert the indigenous people to their own religion, Roman Catholicism. An Aztec man named Juan Diego became one of the first to willingly accept this faith. Juan Diego is at the center of one of Mexico's most important religious stories.

Opposite: **Guadalajara Cathedral was first built in the 1500s, but it has been rebuilt and repaired many times because of earthquake damage.**

The Story of Juan Diego

It is said that on December 9, 1531, Juan Diego headed out to attend church. But on Tepeyac Hill near Mexico City, he was stunned by a vision. Before him, surrounded by light, he saw the Virgin Mary, the mother of Jesus. She was of dark complexion and resembled an Aztec princess. Mary told him to ask the local bishop, a Catholic official, to build a church on the site.

The original image of Our Lady of Guadalupe is housed in a large church that was built especially for it.

Religions of Mexico (2010 est.)

Roman Catholic	82.7%
Pentecostal	1.6%
Jehovah's Witnesses	1.4%
Other Protestant faiths	5.0%
Other religions	1.9%
No religion	4.7%
Unknown	2.7%

Juan Diego did as Mary asked, but the bishop thought he was making up the story. He insisted Juan Diego provide proof that he had seen the vision. Three days passed, and Mary appeared before Juan Diego again. She told him to pick roses from the hillside and take them to the bishop.

Juan Diego gathered the flowers and wrapped them in his cloak. When he opened his cloak before the bishop, Mary's image miraculously appeared on the cloth. Seeing the image as a sign, the bishop had a church constructed to honor the Virgin Mary at the spot where Juan Diego had first seen her.

This traditional story explains how the Basilica of Our Lady of Guadalupe, one of the most sacred places in Mexico, came to be built. Today, millions of Mexicans visit the church every year to pray to Our Lady of Guadalupe. Many approach crawling on their knees to show their devotion.

Our Lady of Guadalupe is more than a religious figure. To some she represents the Aztec mother goddess Tonantzin, or Mother Earth. To most, she has become a symbol of the country itself. Her image can be seen everywhere as evidence of the enormous influence of Catholicism in Mexican life.

Catholic Beliefs and Rituals

About 83 percent of the people of Mexico are Catholics. Catholicism is one branch of Christianity, which follows the teachings of Jesus Christ, who lived about two thousand years ago. These teachings are recounted in the New Testament of the Bible.

A person prays at a church in Mexico City. Roughly half the population of Mexicans attend church services regularly.

A Catholic priest baptizes a baby boy at the cathedral in Mexico City to welcome the child into the faith.

Like other Christians, Catholics believe in one God and that Jesus was his son. Catholicism teaches that after death, believers will go to heaven, as long as they have received God's forgiveness for their sins, or wrongdoings.

The Catholic church service is called Mass. It is overseen by a priest. Priests are men who have devoted their lives to the Church. Women cannot be priests, but they can become nuns. Neither priests nor nuns are allowed to marry.

An important rite in Catholicism is called baptism. Priests baptize babies by sprinkling holy water on their heads. Through baptism, children formally become members of the

Catholic Church. Later, usually as an adolescent, they go through the sacrament of Confirmation, during which they affirm their belief in the Catholic faith.

The Pope is the head of the Catholic Church. The Pope and other Church leaders live in the Vatican, an independent city within Rome, Italy. The Pope's statements about faith and morality have a great influence over the lives of Catholics worldwide.

Sor Juana

A Catholic nun named Juana Inés de la Cruz was one of the greatest Mexican scholars during the Spanish colonial period.

Probably born in 1651, Sor Juana taught herself to read in her grandfather's library when she was three years old. When her grandfather died, Juana was sent to live with relatives in Mexico City. As a young woman, she was not allowed to attend the university there, so she devoted herself to studying theology, astronomy, philosophy, and a host of other subjects on her own.

Juana decided she did not want to marry. In 1669, she entered a convent to become a nun. She became known as Sor Juana (Sister Juana). At the convent, Sor Juana amassed some four thousand books. Her library was one of the biggest in North America. She also wrote poetry and plays. Sor Juana became famous for her writings in both Mexico and Spain.

Sor Juana died of the plague in 1695 while nursing her fellow nuns during an epidemic. Now celebrated for her remarkable life and career, Sor Juana appears on Mexico's 200-peso banknote.

Patron Saints

Saints are also important in the Catholic faith. They are people who, after their death, the Church reveres for having lived especially virtuous lives. Juan Diego, for instance, was made a saint in 2002. Catholics pray to saints to ask for their help. They also visit shrines dedicated to specific saints. Shrines contain paintings and sculptures of saints and objects associated with them. The shrine of Our Lady of Guadalupe holds Juan Diego's cloak marked with the image of Mary.

Some pilgrims walk for days to reach the Basilica of Our Lady of Guadalupe in time for the feast day honoring the figure on December 12. Many pilgrims carry icons, or images, of Our Lady of Guadalupe on their journey.

Until recently, nearly all Mexican children were baptized in the name of a saint. That saint remained special to them throughout their lives. The Church assigns one day out of the year to each saint. It is called the saint's feast day. People celebrate the feast day associated with their saint almost like a second birthday.

Every Mexican city, town, and neighborhood also has its own patron saint. On their saint's feast day, towns often hold processions, during which a statue of the saint is carried through the streets. The festivities might also include music, dancing, and fireworks. The biggest feast day celebration is held on December 12. On that day, nearly everyone in Mexico honors the Virgin of Guadalupe, the country's patron saint.

Parachicos dancers are a traditional part of the festival honoring Sebastian, the patron saint of the town of Chiapa de Corzo. The dancers wear wooden masks and headdresses made from the fibers of the agave plant.

On Palm Sunday, some Mexicans carry woven palm fronds adorned with images of Our Lady of Guadalupe.

Easter and Christmas

Other important Catholic holidays in Mexico are clustered around Easter and Christmas celebrations. The observances held during Semana Santa—Holy Week, the week leading up to Easter Sunday—vary from location to location. On Palm Sunday (the Sunday before Easter), many towns hold processions that reenact Jesus's arrival in Jerusalem on the back of a donkey. On Holy Saturday (the day before Easter), many Mexicans hold a joyous festival during which a dummy of Judas, who betrayed Jesus, is set ablaze with fireworks. Easter Sunday, marking the day Jesus is said to have risen to heaven, is much more somber. Usually, people attend Mass with their families.

The Christmas season begins with the Posadas, a nine-

Religious Holidays in Mexico

Three Kings' Day (Epiphany)	January 6
Candlemas	February 2
Good Friday	March or April
Easter	March or April
Corpus Christi	May or June
St. John the Baptist Day	June 24
All Saints' Day	November 1
All Souls' Day (Day of the Dead)	November 2
Our Lady of Guadalupe Day	December 12
The Posadas	December 16–24
Christmas Day	December 25

day celebration beginning December 16. People reenact the arrival in Bethlehem of Mary and Joseph, the parents of Jesus, before his birth. Posadas are often festive and include piñatas, tamales, and sweet drinks. On Christmas Eve, many Mexicans attend Mass at midnight. Children receive gifts on Christmas Eve or Christmas Day. They open presents again on Epiphany, which falls on January 6. This celebration commemorates the Three Kings' journey to see the baby Jesus.

Other Faiths

The vast majority of Mexicans consider themselves Catholic. Many Mexican Catholics are devout. They attend Mass regularly, celebrate religious holidays, and visit sacred sites. Some Mexican Catholics are not so traditional. They might go to Mass occasionally. The number of Mexican Catholics is falling. In 1970, about 96 percent of the population embraced Catholicism. By 2010, about 83 percent did.

Mexican worshippers attend an evangelical service in León. Some people are drawn to evangelical churches because their services are more active and openly emotional than Catholic services.

About 5 percent of Mexicans do not belong to any organized religion. Mexico is also home to small numbers of Jews, Muslims, Buddhists, and Hindus. Still others are Christians who belong to various Protestant faiths. These include Pentecostals, Jehovah's Witnesses, Presbyterians, Methodists, Baptists, and Mormons (members of the Church of Jesus Christ of Latter-day Saints). Many of them are recent converts who were exposed to Protestantism by missionaries from the United States.

Some people belong to newer religions that originated in Mexico. La Luz del Mundo (Light of the World) was founded in the city of Monterrey by Eusebio Joaquín González in 1926. Calling himself the Apostle Aarón, he steadily attracted followers. Many of them moved to a religious community named Hermosa Provincia near Guadalajara. According to the 2010 census, about 188,000 Mexicans belong to the religion but the church claims the number is much higher.

Mexico has also recently seen the rise of the Santa Muerte (Saint Death) cult. Many people who have embraced it are poor and desperate, including many men in prison. Cult members pray to Santa Muerte, whom they envision as the skeleton of a woman wrapped in robes. The faithful use elements of Catholic rituals when worshipping their self-created saint. Now often embraced by gang members, Santa Muerte is highly controversial in Mexico. Even so, this fast-growing movement continues to attract new believers, both in and outside of Mexico.

Healing the Sick

The traditional religious beliefs of the indigenous peoples of Mexico still have an influence over Mexican life, particularly in rural areas. For instance, many people seek the help of a *curandero* if they become ill. Curanderos are traditional healers who use lotions, herbs, and charms to cure their patients. They are thought to inherit their spiritual power, so often there are several generations of curanderos within the same family.

CHAPTER 9

Mexican Creativity

SOME THE MOST TREASURED WORKS OF MEXICAN art were created hundreds or thousands of years ago. Artists of the Olmec civilization crafted small human sculptures from clay and carved enormous busts in stone. The Mayas made books from folded bark and painted colorful murals on the walls of their buildings. The Aztecs created jewelry from gold, silver, and jade and fashioned brilliant feathers into head-dresses and cloaks.

Opposite: **This Mayan figure of a ball player dates to between 700 and 900 CE. The figure is wearing heavy protective gear.**

Templo Mayor

On February 21, 1978, a group of workers for an electric company made an amazing discovery in the middle of Mexico City. They unearthed a stone disc 10.5 feet (3.2 m) across. It was carved with a strange and gory image—a woman's body with her head, arms, and legs cut off.

The carving represents Coyolxauhqui, a moon goddess worshipped by the Aztecs. Coyolxauhqui was killed by her brother Huitzilopochtli, the Aztec god of war. In his honor, the ancient Aztecs constructed Templo Mayor (Main Temple).

After the accidental discovery of this long-buried monument, the Mexican government began a massive project to uncover the temple at the site. Visitors can now walk along raised platforms and look down into the archaeological site. They can also visit a museum displaying art and artifacts found there. Among the more than seven thousand objects are sculptures, tools, bowls, and jewelry. The excavation of Templo Mayor continues, with the promise of many more treasures to come.

Creating a Mexican Style

These ancient artworks inspired some of the most famous works of twentieth-century Mexican art. In the 1920s, Mexico's education minister José Vasconcelos hired several painters to create murals in public buildings. Muralists Diego Rivera, José Clemente Orozco, and David Alfaro Siqueiros drew from Mexico's past artistic traditions to create a new art style. Full of color and crowded with figures and images, their murals depicted events in the country's history from a distinctly Mexican perspective.

Some artists of the 1950s and 1960s, such as José Luis Cuevas and Francisco Toledo, rejected the style that the muralists had pioneered. Calling themselves the Generación de la Ruptura (Breakaway Generation), they began creating more abstract paintings, drawing on European modern art. Another contemporary Mexican artist of note is Sebastian. His monumental concrete and steel sculptures are displayed throughout the world.

José Clemente Orozco painted bold figures to represent the struggles of the poor and powerless.

In recent decades, Mexico City has become a vital art center. It has many galleries and museums that display works of fine art from the past and present. Each February, the city hosts Zona Maco, a five-day art fair that brings the public together with Mexico's many working artists.

Folk Art

Some Mexican artists make their living producing traditional handicrafts. They make pottery, baskets, and weavings. Many artisans also craft masks out of leather, wood, and papier-

Frida Kahlo

Painter Frida Kahlo used her self-portraits to explore both Mexican culture and her own personal struggles and pain. At nineteen, she was riding in a bus when it was struck by a trolley car. The accident fractured her spine and broke bones throughout her body. Her injuries left her with deep, chronic pain.

After recuperating, Kahlo took up painting. Most of her works were small self-portraits, highlighting her large eyes and thick eyebrows. She often surrounded her face with objects and adornments relating to Mexican history and the Catholic religion.

In 1929, Kahlo married the muralist Diego Rivera. The couple's relationship was stormy, but it brought her in contact with many of the leading artists and thinkers of her time.

Kahlo had her first one-woman show in 1953, a year before she died at forty-seven. Her fame has only grown since her death. Kahlo is not only one of Mexico's best-loved artists but also one of the most famous female painters in the world.

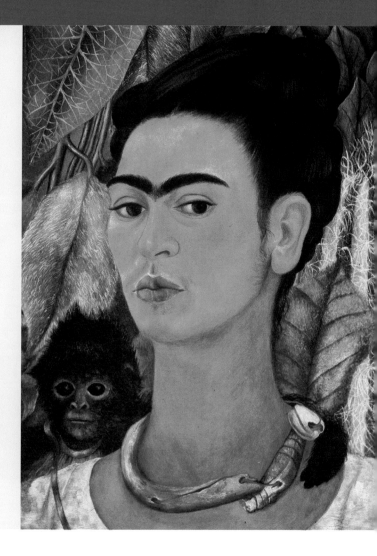

mâché. They sell their masks to tourists and other revelers during festivals. Some city and state governments sponsor folk art contests with cash prizes.

The Huichol Indians of the Sierra Madre Occidental are known for their yarn paintings. Huichol artists make them by pressing colorful strands of yarn onto boards coated with sticky wax. Their vibrant designs are inspired by visions of traditional Huichol spiritual leaders. Huichol yarn paintings today are sought by art collectors from around the world.

In southern Mexico, many folk artists create brightly colored sculptures of fantastical creatures called *alebrijes.*

Another popular type of Mexican folk art is the *árbol de la vida,* or tree of life. Artists in the town of Metepec in central Mexico are particularly well known for their tree of life sculptures. These large clay works feature many small figures and animals, all molded by hand. Many trees of life depict the Biblical story of Adam and Eve in the Garden of Eden.

Mariachi performers in Mexico City. The mariachi tradition emerged in western Mexico in the 1700s. It has changed over the centuries, incorporating different types of music and becoming a symbol of Mexico.

Traditional Songs

Mexico is filled with the sound of music. Songs blast out of the radios of passing cars and buses. Musicians play in town squares. Bands wander through restaurants, stopping to play at tables in exchange for a modest tip.

Like so much of Mexican culture, the country's music shows both Indian and Spanish influences. The first people of Mexico played music on drums, flutes, and rattles. After the arrival of the Spanish, Mexican musicians began playing European instruments, such as the harp, violin, and guitar. The most distinctively Mexican music makes use of some combination of all these instruments.

Son—the Spanish word for sound—is one type of Mexican folk music. Son songs are played with percussion and stringed instruments. Their lyrics often tell stories of love or tales of legendary figures. The traditional dance performed to son music is the *zapateado*. Dancers tap their shoes and stomp their feet to emphasize certain beats.

Ranchera music had its beginnings in the years following the Mexican Revolution. Its emotional songs deal with rural life in Mexico's northern ranch lands. Vicente Fernández, the most famous ranchera singer, was dubbed El Rey (the King) by his millions of fans.

Corrido is another type of Mexican folk song. Men traditionally sang these ballads while strumming a guitar. The songs told stories, often about a hero's adventures or a bandit's crimes.

One of Mexico's best-known contributions to music is the mariachi band. In these bands, singers are accompanied by guitars, violins, and trumpets. All the band members traditionally wear matching *charro* suits. Based on garb worn by cowherds, the suits have short jackets and high-waisted pants. Often, mariachi musicians top off their look by wearing traditional wide-brimmed hats called sombreros.

Modern Music

In addition to traditional songs, Mexicans enjoy just about every modern musical style, from rock to hip-hop and from metal to ska. Young people in cities also enjoy dancing in nightclubs, often to salsa or reggae.

Much of the popular music heard in Mexico is imported

Some traditional Mexican dancers wear brightly colored dresses with full skirts.

from other countries. But many Mexican musical acts have loyal followings at home and beyond. Already famous as a television actress, Thalía has had an enormous second career as a pop singer, selling some forty million albums worldwide. Maná, one of Mexico's most popular rock bands, found international fame in the 1990s. Their record *¿Dónde jugarán los niños?* (*Where Will the Children Play?*) held the number one spot on *Billboard* magazine's Latin American album chart for almost one hundred weeks. Called the Sun of Mexico, Luis Miguel is revered as a singer and a showman. His concert tours bring out Spanish-speaking fans around the globe. Juan Gabriel, who died in 2016, was an iconic musical figure known worldwide for his flamboyant style and singing talent.

Octavio Paz was considered a master poet. He was deeply interested in philosophy and politics, and his work was unusual in that it sometimes blended the form of a poem with the content of an essay.

Literature and Film

Mexico has a strong literary tradition. The country has produced many noted essayists, poets, and novelists. Among Mexico's most celebrated writers is Octavio Paz. One of his best-known books is *The Labyrinth of Solitude* (1950), an exploration of the character of the Mexican people. In 1990, Paz was awarded the Nobel Prize in Literature.

Other important Mexican authors include Carlos Fuentes and Laura Esquivel. Fuentes's novel *The Death of Artemio Cruz* tells of the life and times of a soldier in the Mexican Revolution. Laura Esquivel had a best seller with *Like Water for Chocolate*. The love story includes a recipe at the beginning of each chapter.

A young man plays basketball on a cloudy day in southern Mexico.

The Mexican film industry had its golden age in the 1930s and 1940s. But in recent years, it has once again drawn international attention, largely due to the work of three Mexican directors—Alfonso Cuarón, Guillermo del Toro, and Alejandro Iñárritu. Both Cuarón (*Gravity*, 2013) and Iñárritu (*Birdman*, 2014; *The Revenant*, 2015) have won the Academy Award for Best Director.

In Spanish-speaking countries, Mexico has also made its mark on television by pioneering the telenovela. Telenovelas are melodramatic serialized dramas that often focus on a beautiful female heroine. Millions of Mexicans turn on their televisions at the same time each evening to catch up on their favorite stories.

Sports

Many Mexicans enjoy both playing and watching sports. Basketball, volleyball, boxing, and especially baseball are popular. Several Mexican athletes have been drafted by major league baseball teams in the United States. Golf and tennis are played at private clubs, but only wealthy Mexicans have enough money to join them.

Mexicans living along both coasts like to go swimming. Other water sports include scuba diving, surfing, and snorkeling. In the resort city of Acapulco, professional divers jump into the Pacific Ocean from 150-foot-high (46 m) cliffs as paying tourists watch.

But Mexico's favorite sport by far is soccer. The Mexican soccer league has eighteen teams. The most anticipated

El César

One of the all-time greats in the sport of boxing, Julio César Chávez was born in 1962 in northern Mexico. He took up boxing early during trips to the gym with his older brothers. Chávez won his first professional fight at seventeen.

Chávez quickly emerged as a world-class athlete. In a particularly dramatic bout, he took on Edwin Rosario, a Puerto Rican boxer who had made insulting comments about Mexicans before the fight. Chávez landed the majority of his punches, winning him both the world lightweight championship and the devotion of the Mexican people. Another memorable fight was against American Meldrick Taylor in 1990. After taking a vicious beating, Chávez was poised to lose, when, with twelve seconds left, he delivered a knockout punch, snatching victory.

Known as El César del Boxeo to his fans, Chávez

earned six world championships during his twenty-five-year career. Before retiring in 2006, he won a total of 107 fights, including 89 in a row—the longest winning streak in boxing history.

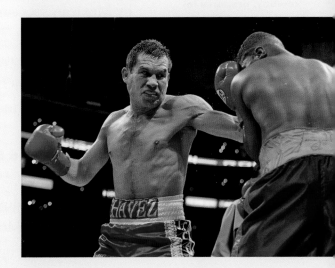

A Mexican *charro*, or cowboy, prepares to lasso a horse during a charreada rodeo competition.

matchup is El Súper Clásico (the Super Classic). It is played by Mexican soccer's most popular teams and greatest rivals— Chivas from Guadalajara and Club América from Mexico City. Mexico's national team regularly participates in international tournaments, including the World Cup. The country has also hosted the World Cup finals twice, in 1970 and 1986.

Bullfighting and Horse Riding

Some five hundred years ago, the Spanish introduced Mexico to bullfighting. Mexico today has the largest bullfighting ring in the world. La Monumental in Mexico City seats more than forty thousand people.

During a bullfight, a man called a matador waves a red cape to provoke a bull into charging. The matador then must dodge the bull or end up being gored by the animal's horns. At the end of the fight, the bull is killed.

Bullfighting is now controversial in Mexico. Some people believe it is an important part of Mexican culture. Others denounce the sport because it is cruel to animals.

In northern Mexico, competitors show off their ranching and horse riding skills at *charreadas*, which are similar to American rodeos. Teams compete in ten events, including steer wrestling, bull roping, and riding bucking horses. One event features women on horseback performing a choreographed program to music.

Lucha Libre

For many Mexicans, the best show in town is not found on a concert stage or in a theater. It is at a sports arena, whenever *lucha libre* is on the schedule.

Translating literally as "free wrestling," lucha libre was invented by Salvador Lutteroth in 1933. Inspired by professional wrestling in the United States, he established in Mexico City a small venue where men could wrestle before a crowd. The new sport was an instant success. Within a year, the wrestlers—called *luchadores*—were performing in huge arenas filled with thousands of spectators.

In the ring, luchadores wear wrestling tights and brightly colored masks. The wrestling moves are worked out in advance, making lucha libre more of a performance than a sport. Each wrestler also takes on a personality, with some being heroes and others villains. Lucha libre fans enjoy being part of the show as they cheer or boo the appearance of their favorite characters.

CHAPTER 10

The Mexican Way of Life

I N MODERN MEXICO, THERE IS NO SINGLE MEXICAN
way of life. The daily life of different Mexicans varies tremen-
dously. Where people live has a big impact on how they live.
People in different regions of Mexico often have different
customs. People's incomes also determine their daily routines.
More than half the people in Mexico are poor. Their life has
little in common with the luxurious life of Mexico's wealthy.

Opposite: **Young Mexicans
wait in line to enter an art
exhibit in Mexico City.**

Rural and Urban

Whether a person lives in the country or the city has a large
impact on their daily life. About 80 percent of Mexicans live
in cities and towns. Only one out of five lives in a rural area.

Many people in the countryside are poor, and often
they are of Indian descent. They generally make a living by
farming, although they often do not own their own land.

A Maya woman stands in the door of her house. The roof is made with the fronds of palm leaves.

Grandparents, parents, and children live together in clusters of small buildings. These modest houses are usually built from clay, wood, or concrete. They might have dirt floors and contain just a few pieces of furniture.

Rural Mexicans generally hold on to older traditions more than city dwellers. They are likely to eat the same kinds of foods and take part in the same ceremonies as their ancestors did.

In cities, many workers live in apartments. Wealthier people might have small houses. The very rich live in mansions with large household staffs.

The poorest city dwellers often struggle to find a decent place to live. The government has built some small houses on the edge of cities for poor workers. But there are not enough government houses for everyone who needs them.

Many people have no choice but to live in shantytowns. These makeshift settlements lie outside of cities. People in shantytowns build their own houses out of whatever they can find, including sheets of metal, plywood, or cardboard.

Family Life

No matter where they live, most Mexicans share a deep love for their families. Several generations of relatives usually live close to one another, if not in the same house. Often, young adults are in no hurry to move from their parents' house, and parents are also in no hurry to send them off on their own.

Two young girls enjoy a ride on the back of their father's bicycle. The average Mexican family has two children.

The Blind Hen

A favorite game of Mexican children is *la gallinita ciega*, or the blind hen. It is like blind man's bluff. A scarf is tied over the eyes of one player, the hen. The other players turn the hen around several times and then begin calling out to him or her. Guided by their voices, the hen, with arms outstretched, tries to grab one of the players. When grabbed, that player then becomes the new hen, and the game continues.

People feel an obligation to older relatives. They treat them with respect and care for them in their old age. Mexicans also tend to dote on their children. The family lavishes the children with time and attention.

Traditionally, Mexican women, like most women in the world, were homemakers. But many now have jobs outside

A grandmother holds up her grandson. The life expectancy for Mexican women is seventy-nine years and for men it is seventy-three years.

The Quinceañera Celebration

When a girl turns fifteen in Mexico, she often experiences one of the most memorable birthdays of her life. By tradition, that birthday is marked by a great celebration called a quinceañera.

Quinceañeras are held in many Spanish-speaking countries, as well as in Hispanic communities in the United States. But the ceremony probably had its origins in Mexico's ancient Aztec civilization. These early quinceañeras were intended to prepare young women for marriage. Modern quinceañeras generally mark the point at which young women are allowed to start dating.

In Mexico, the celebration begins with a Catholic Mass. Afterward, the birthday girl's friends and relatives gather for a party. The honored girl wears an elaborate gown in a color of her choosing. Her closest friends wear coordinated clothing in the same color.

Quinceañeras include much food, music, and dancing, as well as several unique rituals. For instance, the hosts might bring out fifteen piñatas, one for each

year in the girl's life. Sometimes, the birthday girl is presented with her "last doll." She then gives the doll to a younger female relative as a symbol that her own girlhood has come to an end.

the home. Working mothers sometimes rely on grandparents to care for their children. But even when women hold a job, they still do most of the housework. They might have help from older daughters or, if the family makes enough money, a hired maid.

In recent times, many Mexicans have had to move to cities or even the United States to find work. But even if they live far away, they try to stay in touch with their families. Often, they will send relatives money and visit their family whenever they can.

When not at work, most Mexicans spend much of their time with relatives. Family members might visit a park, have a picnic, take in a movie, or go to the beach. Families often spend public holidays together. They also gather to celebrate births, birthdays, feast days, and funerals.

Weddings are particularly important family events. During the ceremony, the groom presents the bride with thirteen gold coins as a symbol of his love. To signify their bond, their wrists are wrapped together by a white ribbon or a rosary (Catholic prayer beads). Guests toss red beads at the couple as a way of wishing them good luck.

A boy swings a stick at a piñata. The history of piñatas can be traced to both Aztec and European traditions. In Mexico, piñatas are common during the days before Christmas as well as on birthdays.

Food and Drink

At almost any Mexican celebration, food and drink take center stage. Traditional Mexican dishes feature foods native to the region, such as corn, chilies, turkey, and chocolate. They are often combined with foods introduced by the Spanish, including beef, onions, wheat, and milk. The result is a very tasty cuisine.

Many Mexican dishes feature tortillas. These flat discs of bread are made from cornmeal or wheat flour. Tacos are tortillas filled with meat, fish, or vegetables. Quesadillas are folded tortillas stuffed with cheese, meat, or another filling. Enchiladas are fried tortillas rolled around a filling and covered with sauce.

A Mayan woman makes tortillas.

Agua Fresca

When the temperature rises, Mexicans cool off with refreshing *agua fresca*. Spanish for "fresh water," an agua fresca is made from fresh fruit blended with water, sugar, and sometimes grain, seeds, or even flowers. Mexicans often buy these drinks from street vendors or at outdoor markets. But you can easily make one yourself in your kitchen. Have an adult help you.

Ingredients

1 cup of fruit
2 cups of water
2 tablespoons of sugar
Lime wedges or mint leaves (optional)

Directions

Choose fruit such as mangoes, strawberries, watermelons, cantaloupes, or papayas, and cut into cubes. Place the fruit, water, and sugar in a blender. Blend until smooth. Pour the drink into four tall glasses filled with ice. If you like, add a lime wedge or a few mint leaves for extra flavor. Enjoy!

Many of the signature dishes of Mexico feature some variety of *mole*. Mole is a sauce made from some combination of spices, nuts, and chilies that is served over turkey, chicken, or pork. Some moles also include chocolate.

Since the time of the Aztecs, chocolate-flavored drinks have been popular in Mexico. Mexicans also enjoy soft drinks called *refrescos* and milkshakes made with fruit, called *licuados*.

Mexicans usually have their main meal, called *comida*, in the middle of the afternoon. Small family-owned restaurants called *fondas* often offer three-course comidas at an inexpensive fixed price. *Cena*, the Mexican dinner, is much lighter. It is served after the workday, sometimes as late as ten o'clock at night.

Before going out in the evening, people might grab a few small bites called *antojitos* at street stalls. After a long night on the town, they also often stop at a *taqueria* for a taco before going home.

Holidays and Festivals

Mexicans come together for many Catholic observances throughout the year. But they also celebrate a wide array of public holidays and festivals.

Several cities in Mexico host Carnival celebrations in February or March. Stretching over five to nine days and nights, Carnival brings crowds out into the streets for parades, concerts, and fireworks. The city of Mazatlán is particularly known for its street festival, which attracts some three hundred thousand partiers each year.

A horseman dressed in a traditional charro outfit takes part in a large military parade in Mexico City celebrating Independence Day.

The San Marcos Fair is held over three weeks each spring. Hosted by the city of San Marcos in central Mexico, this enormous fair features music, dancing, art exhibits, bullfighting, and rodeo competitions. Another highly anticipated event is La Noche de los Rábanos, or the Night of the Radishes. On December 23, the city square in Oaxaca is decorated with large radishes carved into human figures, animals, and other shapes. Visitors can buy the radish carvings to use as centerpieces for their Christmas dinner table.

The entire country joins in celebrating several days each year that commemorate important people and events in Mexico's history. Every March 21, Mexicans celebrate the birthday of Benito Juárez, the nineteenth-century president who is now considered a national hero. Cinco de Mayo, or the Fifth of May, honors a small force of Mexican fighters who

National Holidays

New Year's Day	January 1
Constitution Day	February 5
Birthday of Benito Juárez	March 21
Labor Day	May 1
Independence Day	September 16
Revolution Day	November 20
Christmas	December 25

defeated the French army at the Battle of Puebla in 1862. This holiday is now also celebrated in Mexican-American communities in the United States.

But Mexico's most important patriotic holiday falls on September 16. It commemorates the day in 1810 when Father Miguel Hidalgo called for his fellow Mexicans to join him in rising up against Spanish rule. Considered Mexico's Independence Day, it is celebrated with parades, brass bands, flag waving, and fireworks. People also enjoy a special holiday treat called *chiles en nogada*. It is made from stuffed green chilies topped with walnut sauce and pomegranate seeds. Colored green, white, and red, it recalls the stripes of the Mexican flag.

The Independence Day festivities begin the night before. Throughout Mexico, people gather in their city squares, waiting for the local mayors to reenact Hidalgo's *grito*, or cry, to fight for freedom. The biggest crowd is in Mexico City. There, the president of Mexico emerges from the balcony of the National Palace. He rings a replica of Hidalgo's bell and yells out the words that have long expressed Mexicans' deep love and hope for their country: "Long live Mexico! Long live Mexico! Long live Mexico!"

Timeline

MEXICAN HISTORY

Human beings in what is now Mexico learn to farm.	**ca. 9000 BCE**
The Aztecs found their capital city of Tenochtitlán.	**1325 CE**
Hernán Cortés leads a force that conquers the Aztec Empire.	**1521**
Father Miguel Hidalgo calls for Mexicans to rise up against Spanish rule.	**1810**
Mexico becomes an independent nation.	**1821**
Mexico loses half its territory to the United States after its defeat in the Mexican-American War.	**1848**

WORLD HISTORY

ca. 2500 BCE	The Egyptians build the pyramids and the Sphinx in Giza.
ca. 563 BCE	The Buddha is born in India.
313 CE	The Roman emperor Constantine legalizes Christianity.
610	The Prophet Muhammad begins preaching a new religion called Islam.
1054	The Eastern (Orthodox) and Western (Roman Catholic) Churches break apart.
1095	The Crusades begin.
1215	King John seals the Magna Carta.
1300s	The Renaissance begins in Italy.
1347	The plague sweeps through Europe.
1453	Ottoman Turks capture Constantinople, conquering the Byzantine Empire.
1492	Columbus arrives in North America.
1500s	Reformers break away from the Catholic Church, and Protestantism is born.
1776	The U.S. Declaration of Independence is signed.
1789	The French Revolution begins.

MEXICAN HISTORY

France invades Mexico City and installs Ferdinand Maximilian as emperor of Mexico.	**1863**
Porfirio Díaz becomes president.	**1876**
The Mexican Revolution begins.	**1910**
Mexico adopts the constitution that established its modern government.	**1917**
The party now known as the Institutional Revolutionary Party (PRI) is founded and begins its domination of Mexican politics.	**1929**
Mexican police and soldiers shoot student demonstrators in Mexico City.	**1968**
Oil reserves are found off the coast of Mexico.	**1976**
The North American Free Trade Agreement (NAFTA) is passed.	**1994**
Vicente Fox of the National Action Party is elected president, ending the PRI's control of the presidency.	**2000**
The government declares war on drug traffickers, leading to a new wave of violence in the drug trade.	**2006**
Enrique Peña Nieto is elected president, restoring the PRI to power.	**2012**
Forty-three college students are kidnapped, possibly by drug traffickers.	**2014**

WORLD HISTORY

1865	The American Civil War ends.
1879	The first practical lightbulb is invented.
1914	World War I begins.
1917	The Bolshevik Revolution brings communism to Russia.
1929	A worldwide economic depression begins.
1939	World War II begins.
1945	World War II ends.
1969	Humans land on the Moon.
1975	The Vietnam War ends.
1989	The Berlin Wall is torn down as communism crumbles in Eastern Europe.
1991	The Soviet Union breaks into separate states.
2001	Terrorists attack the World Trade Center in New York City and the Pentagon near Washington, D.C.
2004	A tsunami in the Indian Ocean destroys coastlines in Africa, India, and Southeast Asia.
2008	The United States elects its first African American president.
2016	Donald Trump is elected U.S. president.

Fast Facts

Official name: Estados Unidos Mexicanos
(United Mexican States)

Capital: Mexico City

Official language: None

Mexico City

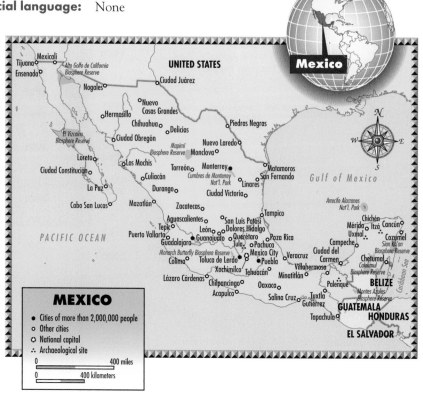

MEXICO

- ● Cities of more than 2,000,000 people
- ○ Other cities
- ✪ National capital
- ∴ Archaeological site

National flag

Baja California

Official religion:	None
Year of founding:	1821
National anthem:	"Himno Nacional Mexicano" ("National Anthem of Mexico")
Government:	Federal presidential republic
Head of state:	President
Head of government:	President
Area of country:	758,449 square miles (1,964,375 sq km)
Latitude and longitude of geographic center:	23°00' N, 102°00' W
Bordering countries:	United States to the north, Guatemala and Belize to the south
Highest elevation:	Pico de Orizaba, 18,619 feet (5,675 m) above sea level
Lowest elevation:	Laguna Salada, 33 feet (10 m) below sea level
Average high temperature:	In Mexico City, 81°F (27°C) in May; 72°F (22°C) in December
Average low temperature:	In Mexico City, 54°F (12°C) in May; 43°F (6°C) in December
Average annual rainfall:	28 inches (71 cm) in Mexico City

Uxmal

Currency

National population (2016 est.): 123,155,749

Population of major cities (2015 est.):

Mexico City	20,999,000
Guadalajara	4,843,000
Monterrey	4,513,000
Puebla	2,984,000
Toluca de Lerdo	2,164,000

Landmarks:
- ▶ *Copper Canyon,* Chihuahua
- ▶ *Degollado Theater,* Guadalajara
- ▶ *National Palace,* Mexico City
- ▶ *Templo Mayor,* Mexico City
- ▶ *Uxmal,* Yucatán

Economy: Traditionally, Mexico's economy was based on agriculture and ranching. Today, most Mexican workers have jobs in the service and manufacturing industries. Since the North American Free Trade Agreement (NAFTA) went into effect in 1994, the United States has been Mexico's most important trading partner. Mexico's lucrative oil fields are managed by the state-owned corporation Pemex. The country also has substantial deposits of silver, copper, and iron.

Currency: The peso. In 2017, US$1 equaled about 21 pesos.

System of weights and measures: Metric system

Literacy rate: 95%

Schoolgirl

Frida Kahlo

Common Spanish words and phrases:

¡Hola!	Hello
Adiós	Good-bye
Buenos días	Good morning
Buenas noches	Good night
Sí	Yes
No	No
Por favor	Please
Gracias	Thank you

Prominent Mexicans:

Julio César Chávez (1962–)
Boxer

Miguel Hidalgo y Costilla (1753–1811)
Priest and revolutionary leader

Alejandro Iñárritu (1963–)
Film director

Juana Inés de la Cruz (ca. 1651–1695)
Nun and writer

Benito Júarez (1806–1872)
President

Frida Kahlo (1907–1954)
Artist

Octavio Paz (1914–1998)
Poet

To Find Out More

Books

- ▶ Baquedano, Elizabeth. *Aztec, Inca & Maya*. New York: DK Publishing, 2011.

- ▶ Carew-Miller, Anna. *Famous People of Mexican History*. Philadelphia: Mason Crest, 2014.

- ▶ Centore, Michael. *Mexico: Tradition, Culture, and Daily Life*. Philadelphia: Mason Crest, 2015.

- ▶ Fabiny, Sarah. *Who Was Frida Kahlo?* New York: Grosset & Dunlap, 2013.

- ▶ Tonatiuh, Duncan. *Funny Bones: Posada and His Day of the Dead Calaveras*. New York: Abrams Books for Young Readers, 2015.

- ▶ Yomtov, Nel. *The United States and Mexico*. New York: Scholastic, 2013.

Music

- ▶ Luis Miguel. *Romances*. Miami Beach: WEA Latina, 2010.

- ▶ Maná. *¿Dónde jugarán los niños?* Mexico City: WM Mexico, 2010.

- ▶ *Putumayo Presents: Mexico*. New York: Putumayo World Music, 2016.

▶ Visit this Scholastic website for more information on Mexico:
www.factsfornow.scholastic.com
Enter the keyword **Mexico**

Index

Page numbers in *italics*
indicate illustrations.

Meet the Author

Liz Sonneborn, a graduate of Swarthmore College, lives in Brooklyn, New York. She has written more than one hundred books for adults and young readers, specializing in biography and American and world history. Her books include *The Ancient Aztecs*, *The Mexican-American War*, *The American West*, and *A to Z of American Indian Women*. Sonneborn is also the author of numerous volumes for the Enchantment of the World Series, including *Yemen*, *Iraq*, *North Korea*, *Pakistan*, *France*, and *Tibet*.

Photo Credits

Photographs ©:

cover: Holly Wilmeth/Getty Images; back cover: Danita Delimont Stock/AWL Images; 2: Efrain Padro/ Alamy Images; 5: Steve Bly/Getty Images; 6 left: Kuryanovich Tatsiana/Shutterstock; 6 right: Hemis/Alamy Images; 6 center: age fotostock/Alamy Images; 7 left: Arco Images GmbH/Alamy Images; 7 right: dbimages/ Alamy Images; 8: Thom_Morris/iStockphoto; 10: Jan Sochor/Alamy Images; 12: National Geographic Creative/Alamy Images; 13: Hemis.fr/Superstock, Inc.; 15: Jan Sochor/age fotostock/Superstock, Inc.; 17: Hemis/Alamy Images; 18: George H.H. Huey/Alamy Images; 21: RangeR/Getty Images; 22: Buddy Mays/ Getty Images; 23 left: Jorge Garrido/Alamy Images; 23 right: Madrugadaverde/Dreamstime; 24: Christian Kober/Getty Images; 26: Kuryanovich Tatsiana/Shutterstock; 27: Franz Marc Frei/LOOK-foto/Getty Images; 28: Photography by Jessie Reeder/Getty Images; 29: Rolf Richardson/Alamy Images; 30: Klein and Hubert/ Minden Pictures; 32: CampPhoto/iStockphoto; 33: TiktaAlik/Getty Images; 34: Michael & Patricia Fogden/Minden Pictures/Superstock, Inc.; 35 top: rook76/Getty Images; 35 bottom: Luis Javier Sandoval Alvarado/Superstock, Inc.; 36: rovingmagpie@flickr.com/Getty Images; 37: Leonora Torres/Rodrigo Medellin; 38: Thomas Marent/ardea.com/Pantheon/Superstock, Inc.; 39: Frans Lanting Studio/Alamy Images; 40: Tuul and Bruno Morandi/Alamy Images; 42 bottom: arturogi/iStockphoto; 43: Stefano Ravera/ Alamy Images; 44: DeAgostini/Superstock, Inc.; 45: D. Bayes/Lebrecht/The Image Works; 48: bpperry/ iStockphoto; 50: Don Klumpp/Alamy Images; 52: The Granger Collection; 53: The Print Collector/Alamy Images; 54: Underwood Photo Archives/Superstock, Inc.; 56: Julius Reque/Getty Images; 57: REUTERS/ Alamy Images; 59: Marco Ugarte/AP Images; 60: stockcam/iStockphoto; 63: REUTERS/Alamy Images; 64: Susana Gonzalez/Bloomberg/Getty Images; 65 top right: age fotostock/Alamy Images; 65 bottom right: Visual & Written/Superstock, Inc.; 66: JAVIER LIRA Notimex/Newscom; 67: Poligrafistka/iStockphoto; 68: REUTERS/Alamy Images; 70: epa european pressphoto agency b.v./Alamy Images; 71: Chico Sanchez/ Alamy Images; 72: Brian Overcast/Alamy Images; 74: REUTERS/Alamy Images; 75: Arco Images GmbH/ Alamy Images; 77: Keith Dannemiller/Alamy Images; 79: ML Harris/Alamy Images; 80: Judy Bellah/age fotostock/Superstock, Inc.; 81: YinYang/iStockphoto; 82: Miguel Sobreira/age fotostock; 84: dbimages/Alamy Images; 85: REUTERS/Alamy Images; 88: mofles/iStockphoto; 89: Charles O. Cecil/Alamy Images; 90: Hemis/Alamy Images; 92: EDU Vision/Alamy Images; 93: REUTERS/Alamy Images; 94: frans lemmens/ Alamy Images; 95: DeAgostini/Superstock, Inc.; 96: Anne Lewis/Alamy Images; 97: age fotostock/Alamy Images; 98: sdstockphoto/iStockphoto; 100: REUTERS/Alamy Images; 101: Charles O. Cecil/Alamy Images; 102: The Granger Collection; 104: National Geographic Creative/Alamy Images; 105: The Granger Collection; 106: The Granger Collection; 107: Jim West/Alamy Images; 108: Hemis/Alamy Images; 110: Kobby Dagan/Alamy Images; 111: Steve Northup/Timepix/The LIFE Images Collection/Getty Images; 112: Aurora Photos/Alamy Images; 113: REUTERS/Alamy Images; 114: Cosmo Condina Mexico/Alamy Images; 115: REUTERS/Alamy Images; 116: Dorothy Alexander/Alamy Images; 118: Pierrette Guertin/ Alamy Images; 119: Margaret Metcalfe/Alamy Images; 120: Eye Ubiquitous/age fotostock; 121: Dieu Nalio Chery/AP Images; 122: VWPics/age fotostock/Superstock, Inc.; 123: francesco de marco/Shutterstock; 124: M.Sobreira/Alamy Images; 126: REUTERS/Alamy Images; 130 left: age fotostock/Alamy Images; 131 top: Poligrafistka/iStockphoto; 131 bottom: George H.H. Huey/Alamy Images; 132 bottom: YinYang/ iStockphoto; 132 top: Tuul and Bruno Morandi/Alamy Images; 133 bottom: The Granger Collection; 133 top: mofles/iStockphoto.

Maps by Mapping Specialists.